Introduction

The first edition of *So Many Fabulous Songs*, a discography and catalogue of songs, was published as a booklet in 1996 and proved popular with fans. This updated version has been expanded substantially, reflecting Loudon's prolific output. It also contains original photographs, comment and analysis from fans, an index of first lines, a catalogue of references, a compendium of quotations from the press and an original interview with Loudon. We hope it will provide an interesting reference book for existing fans, and an useful introduction for anyone unfamiliar with his work.

Inevitably there will be some errors and omissions, which we would welcome being pointed out. For dedicated collectors of facts and figures there are some blank pages at the back for corrections and updates. There is also a contacts page listing Loudon Wainwright websites and contact addresses including our own.

We would to thank everyone who has contributed material to this book, Doug Hand, Linda Haslett, Michael Herbert, Terry Kelly, Richard Kemble, Martin Maguire, André Van den Berg, Lynn Westhead and in particular Caesar Glebbeek, for his interview with Loudon and excellent photographs.

We would also like to thank Tim Chronell, Alan Davidson, Graham Easson, Rick Kulick, Ron Mura, Wolfgang Pieker and Bev Sylvester Evans for their invaluable assistance in preparing the material.

GW00580135

5

Biography

The Early Years

Loudon Wainwright III was breech-born[1] on September 5 1946 in Chapel Hill, North Carolina. His father was Loudon S. Wainwright jr., columnist and editor of Life magazine. His mother Martha T. Wainwright was a yoga teacher. Loudon's grandfather was an insurance salesman, and he is a direct descendent of Peter Stuyvesant, the one-legged Dutch governor of New York. The family moved to Westchester County, NY state[2], but also spent time in London and in Beverly Hills California. When he was nine years old he became infatuated with fellow third-grader Liza Minelli.[3]

He bought his first record "All Shook Up" by Elvis Presley and music started to become very important to him. He was given a guitar in 1960 and began playing renditions of the "Third Man" theme and "Jamaica Farewell". He took a few weeks' lessons at the Mt. Kisco School of Music. Between 1961 and 1965 he attended St Andrew's School for Boys in Middletown Delaware,[4] a private boarding school his father had also attended, and later featured in the film "Dead Poets Society". LWIII survived school despite, or perhaps because of his teenage rebelliousness. He formed a jug-band called the Triaca Company, after the manufacturer's name on the bottom of a jug, and played local dances and clubs. His early musical influences were Louis Prima and his wife, singer Keely Smith, Maria Muldair, Ramblin' Jack Elliot (to whom he owes a lot of his guitar style) and the Jim Kweskin Jugband. But he acquired a new musical model when he saw Bob Dylan at the Newport Folk Festival.

He went to Drama school at Carnegie Mellon in Pittsburgh.[5] Here he met George Gerdes[6] and formed the Alumicron Fab Tabs, a folk group playing the coffee house and basement clubs of Pittsburgh. In 1966 he toured the hills of West Virginia as part of a theatre troupe doing mediaeval Bible plays (in one production Loudon played Christ), and Brecht's "Good Woman of Setzchuan". He dropped out after one and a half years at college in 1967. He was disillusioned with reading playwright's lines and taking directors' instructions and he departed for the counter-culture explosion that was happening in San Francisco. Here he embraced the hippie lifestyle. He went to Golden Gate Park, took LSD and watched Janis Joplin, The Grateful Dead, Quicksilver Messenger Service and Big Brother and the Holding Company. He travelled around the country. In Oklahoma he was picked up for possession of marijuana,[7] which could have sent him to jail for seven years had his father not flown in from London and pulled some 'old boy network' strings with the local judge. His father paid his bail on condition that he paid it back, which meant working at a variety of jobs including movie-house janitor at the Orson Welles cinema, boatyard barnacle-scraper, and cook/dishwasher at New York's first Macrobiotic restaurant, the Paradox on East 7th Street.

One Boy and His Guitar

By 1968 he had all but forgotten his desire to be a musician, but while visiting a friend who had a guitar he started playing around and at the end of his stay had five songs. He began to perform them in local clubs and bars. The first time he

So Many MORE Fabulous Songs

Loudon Wainwright III
The Worksop Manual

Edited by Kevin Harrison and Philip Boxall

To Daniel, Rachel,
Ella, Judith and Irene

BAD *Press*

SO MANY MORE FABULOUS SONGS

Edited by Kevin Harrison and Philip Boxall

Published by BAD *Press*
43 Kingsdown House, London E8 2AS
December 1999
© BAD *Press*

ISBN 0-9527918-3-8

Printed by The Book Factory
35/37 Queensland Road, London N7 7AH

Contents

Your popularity, or sometimes lack of it.
Is there any single reason for it?
"It's not my concern. My job is to write the songs, do the
best shows I can, make the best records I can, do the nicest
interviews I can. And get my ass from A to B. That's my job.
Whether I'm popular in this place is not my concern"

(CG/SMMFS)

was paid was in 1968 by the Students' Union of Brandeis University. He was based in the Boston/Cambridge area of Massachusetts which thrived as a folk centre during the sixties.

He was playing in the Gaslight and Gerdes Folk City in Greenwich Village when record-company scouts were on the lookout for new talent to fill the gap caused by Bob Dylan's mysterious motor-cycle accident, which had put him out of action for a while with a broken neck.[8] Loudon had been taken on as house act at the Gaslight, and was seen by Milt Kramer, who became his manager and was able to secure a record deal with Atlantic in 1969. His first album was a critical success and he was hailed as a 'new Bob Dylan', but he couldn't handle it and retreated to Katonah NY. He grew his hair and a big red beard and made very few personal appearances, much to the dismay of his friends, manager, and record company bosses. Album II came out in 1971. The record company and producer had wanted to use a backing band and strings, but the album was completed with no backing except for harmonica. Like the first album it was a great success and he was hailed as a superstar. He toured Europe in 1971 supporting Buffy Sainte Marie, and The Soft Machine at the Roundhouse, and the Everley Brothers at the Royal Albert Hall.

He had already visited England a year earlier, on honeymoon with his wife Kate McGarrigle, and busked in the streets. He appeared on John Peel's show "in session" and performed "Sink the Bismark", "Schooldays", "Be Careful There's a Baby in the House", "East Indian Princess", and "4 is a Magic Number".

The Big Hit

By 'Album III' in 1972 the record company had got its way and Loudon was backed by White Cloud. Although they only did one gig as a band one track, written in 15 minutes became a novelty hit single,[9] reached number 16 in the US Hit Parade on 17 March 1973 and stayed there for four weeks. In Little Rock Arkansas it actually became Number 1, and remained so for six weeks. He became an "overnight success", taken from airports in limos[10] and courted as a pop-star. Once again he couldn't handle the stress of success and didn't tour or promote the hit record. The ☞

next record was badly recorded in five days. It and Unrequited flopped badly and he was dropped by Columbia.

His son Rufus was born in 1972[11] and his daughter Martha in 1975[12]. By now, however his marriage was falling apart[13]. The Albums T Shirt and Final Exam contained some excellent songs but were badly mixed and didn't do well commercially. His music was still going down well live in London and New York, but he could hardly fill a 400 seat theatre in Chicago.

In 1975 he was seen live in Los Angeles[14] by Larry Gelhart, the writer and producer of the long-running Korean War comedy series M*A*S*H. He thought it would be a great idea to have a singing surgeon in the programme. Loudon played Captain Calvin Spalding MD in only three episodes, but was seen by millions in regularly televised re-runs.

During the 1970s he moved from label to label, selling reasonable numbers of records, but never enough to make him or his record companies rich. Therefore he concentrated on his stage act. "A Live One" was recorded at various concerts in Britain and one in Los Angeles. He couldn't get a record deal and his sister Teddy paid the production costs. He didn't make another record for four years.

Fame and Wealth

In the 1980's however he began to produce what many regard as his finest work. He had a rewarding collaboration with Richard Thompson who produced "Fame and Wealth", (1983) also playing lead guitar on two songs[15]. Thompson went on to produce (with Chaim Tannenbaum) "I'm Alright" (1985) and

"More Love Songs" (1986): both were nominated for Grammy awards[16]. In 1982 he played the lead in the Broadway musical "Pump Boys and Dunettes" for four months and in December his daughter Lucy was born to Suzzy Roche[17]. The 1980s also revived his acting career; he was in his first feature film playing the musical partner of Rebecca DeMornay in "The Slugger's Wife". By this time he was semi resident in Britain[18], living in West Hampstead[19], London NW3.

Therapy

In Britain he could fill concert halls while in the US he was still a small club act.

He was asked by Jasper Carrott, who had been a long term admirer, to be the resident "wiseguy singer songwriter" on his BBC1 show and for eight weeks performed a topical song each Saturday night. Unfortunately he and Jasper didn't entirely hit it off and he wasn't in the next series[20].

In 1989 he co-produced with Chaim Tannenbaum what he considered part of a trilogy, all recorded in London. "Therapy" joined "Fame and Wealth" and "More Love Songs".

Being a Dad

Prompted by his father's terminal illness, and 'the pull' of his children he moved back to the US in 1989. He played a Vietnam vet opposite Robert De Niro in the feature film "Jacknife" with old friend George Gerdes. 1990 saw the start of the commissions from National Public Radio for topical songs. He was asked to write a song about Jesse Helms[21], Republican Senator for North Carolina who was campaigning to stop the National Endowment for the Arts funding a Robert

Biography

Mapplethorpe exhibition in Cincinnati. Since then he has regularly produced topical songs on a range of subjects, and these were brought together on the album "Social Studies" in 1999.

He was taken up by the major labels again in 1992. Paul Conroy used to listen to LWIII when at college and had tried unsuccessfully to sign him up in the 1980s. When he heard that "this adult artist" didn't have a record deal he snapped him up for Richard Branson's Virgin[22] label, under which he made four albums, "History" (1992), "Career Moves"(1993), "Grown Man"and "Little Ship".

The Troubadour

Loudon continued a heavy schedule of live appearances in Europe and the US, also appearing in Melbourne Australia in 1994 and at the Cropredy and Cambridge Folk festivals. His son Rufus[23] had critical success with his first album on Steven Spielberg's "Dreamworks" label. It was produced by the legendary Van Dyke Parks after Loudon had given him a tape to listen to.

"Grown Man" appeared in 1996, and features a duet with daughter Martha in "Father Daughter dialogue. He also had his own TV show, "Loudon and Co." for BBC Scotland, which included stars like James Taylor and Iris Dement, and a song and a dialogue from LWIII.

With the album "Little Ship" (1997) Loudon documented his four year relationship, and its breakdown, with Tracey McLeod[24] (TV and radio presenter)

Following the death of his mother[25] he moved back to Katonah in Westchester County, and he now has homes on Shelter Island and in Brooklyn, New York.

Kevin Harrison, 1999

1 *April Fool's Day Morn*
2 *Westchester County*
3 *Liza*
4 *Schooldays*
5 *Ode to Pittsburgh*
6 *Kings and Queens (1975) and Hey Packy (1976)*
7 *Samson and the Warder*
8 *Talking New Bob Dylan (1992)*
9 *Dead Skunk*
10 *A.M. World*
11 *Dilated to Meet You (1973); Lullaby (1973); Rufus is a Tit Man (1975)*
12 *Pretty Little Martha (1978; Five Years Old (1983)*
13 *Whatever Happened to Us (1975); Reciprocity (1976)*
14 *Hollywood Hopeful (1976)*
15 *Reader and Advisor (1983)*
16 *The Grammy Song (1983)*
17 *Screaming Issue (1985)*
18 *Expatriot (1986)*
19 *Primrose Hill (1997)*
20 *Harry's Wall (1989)*
21 *Jesse Don't Like It (1990)*
22 *Virgin 21*
23 *Rufus is a Tit Man (1975)*
24 *Little Ship*
25 *That Hospital*

My Biggest Fan

My biggest fan
Is a 400 pound man
Who knows how many stones
Hang onto his bones.
And you ask how come but hey look—
His mother was a professional cook,
When he was one his father took off,
It was a trauma that he never shook off,
He was dealt that hand,
My biggest fan.

After the show
Fans say thanks and hello.
They proffer something to sign,
Or deliver a glib line,
And you know there's never any escape
From the fan who wants to give you his tape
But when all of those hounds have all done
In the dressing room there remains but one
And it's my main man,
My biggest fan.

Some fans harrass and stalk,
The big guy likes to talk
He knows every song,
What's been good and gone wrong,
He knows the story of my whole cheesy life,
The name of each kid ex-girlfriend and wife,
Every label that I've ever been on—
Yes he's obsessed but he doesn't fawn
Though he understands, because he's
My biggest fan

Most fans are average guys and gals,
Anxious to be your bosom pals
For a night or for an hour
For a bite or some kind of shower,
They got a plan
You understand.
My fan is so large
He's a one-man entourage
There's much more there to him
Than Tom Dick Harry or Jim
But if you want to know just how big
A fan he is he comes to every gig.
Sometimes I sell out—man that's no sin—
But my fan always manages to squeeze in
He's happy to stand, because he's
My biggest fan

But the biggest surprise
Aside from his size
Is just how hip he is
When it comes to show biz
There's a triumvirate a kind of top three,
Yeah there's Bob then there's Neil then
there's me,
Naturally Bob's number one
The runner up that's Mr Young
I'm Number 3 in command,
But he's still my biggest fan,
Hey I'm his Third Man, but he's still
My biggest fan!

Mr Ambivalent and the 400 pound Man

By Philip Boxall

"Pearlstein, Bernstein, Levitt and Fink
Are not Nordic names I know,
But the trouble is, those girls gee whiz,
Make my juices flo-o-ow"

This small but perfectly formed homage to the exoticism of the Jewish girl is one that strikes a chord with me, who once got a crush on someone sight-unseen on learning that her name was Rubinstein. But it strikes another chord as well:

"Wainwright, Zimmerman, Simon, and Cohen/Are the songwriters for me/But there's one name there, that just won't square/With the others cultural-lee-ee-ee"

In theory it's a mystery that Loudon Wainwright whose work is a beautifully crafted blend of intelligence, wit and linguistic skill, often served up in memorably good tunes should be a relatively esoteric artist that everyone has heard of, vaguely, but whose records relatively few people buy; why isn't he a major star? It is also a mystery that the Macintosh computer is a specialised enthusiasm while Bill Gates' much inferior product has made him the richest man in the world. But there you are—it *is* a mystery.

Someone else, of course, would produce a different list of favourite singer songwriters, all of them more famous and most of them not as good as Loudon. Those of them who started off life as white, middle class, protestant American boys will have shed all traces of that persona at the earliest opportunity and cultivated some image more suited to their trade and to the spirit of the age that spawned them— rebellious anti-hero; bum; misunderstood minority. They will have created for themselves a cultural ambiguity in which they can keep that image safe.

For Mr. Ambivalent the cultural cross-dressing option never was available, because ambivalent he may be, but ambiguous he's not. This college kid, cursed with the gift of fluency, indecently articulate, wanted to tell the truth about himself, and the truth was that he wasn't born in a box-car, wasn't a poor immigrant, had never been busted flat in Baton Rouge, and was temperamentally incapable of pretending that he had. His uncompromising desire to tell the truth and his workman-like approach to his task led him to take for his subjects whatever was to hand, and what was to hand was himself and the little details of his life. Details are only worth describing if you get them right, and he discovered an unerring capacity to get them right which has flourished with the years into an accomplished, sometimes harrowing, public dissection of the meaning of his life.

In *Father Daughter Dialogue* the father responds, rather lamely, on the face of it, to his daughter's charge, "The guy singing the songs ain't me." The daughter's charge is that her father seems to think that simply by being able to describe so beautifully a problem, he is absolved of his responsibility for it. He isn't, and he knows it, but he doesn't exactly say so,

11

instead commenting rather archly "It's just my version, how I feel..." He wouldn't need to add the word "shucks" for us to see that he thinks it wiser to play a little dumb here—a little inarticulacy wouldn't go amiss. It's as though he's learned, at last, that fluent words are apt to sound "a trifle pat". Nobody likes a smartass, and it's a curiously two-edged thing, this fluency. It's the stock-in-trade of salesman, politicians, actors, on and off the stage— all the people we least associate with truth. Can someone be trusted to whom language comes so easily? Don't artists have to struggle to express their truth, stammering and mumbling, searching for the words, which when they at last emerge can only form obscure and puzzling metaphors? And isn't this especially true when we try to speak of pain? Surely pain is expressed in howls and whimpers, stifled cries, not elegantly constructed sentences. "The guy singing the songs ain't me" means, presumably, that art is one thing, life another, and though they may be reunited somewhere else, your art in someone else's life, they remain stubbornly separate in your own. Or to put it another way, just because you can articulate your pain so well it doesn't take the pain away, and it doesn't mean there is no pain.

We can forgive ourselves for letting the art and life distinction slip our minds in Loudon's case, because he does sail his art very close to the wind of his life, tempting, almost provoking us to confuse the two. We can only speculate as to whether this is a deliberate ploy. Is he taking the opportunity to get naked and embarrass us, like a naughty boy showing off to the house-guests, while always keeping handy the figleaf of "the guy singing the songs ain't me", or is there a more compelling reason why he can't stray too far from the literal truth. Does it arise, for example from an Anglo-Saxon literal-mindedness, that distrusts too much invention on the grounds that it's not a million miles from telling lies?

If waspishness is one of the outcomes of his famed ambivalence, the other kind of WASPishness has surely played a role in creating it. Part of the cultural bedrock of the Anglo-Saxon middle class, along with notions of duty and doing the right thing, is the obligation to down-play the emotions, to endure vicissitudes, to codify life into a set of relatively simple rules and orthodoxies in which feelings are too unruly to be admitted. Very often to learn these rules they send their boys to boarding schools, in more or less the same way that the Spartans left their new-born babies on the mountain overnight, to see which ones survived. It's a strange kind of exile from your family, and from the female side, which thereby become both objects of longing and objects of distrust. In this exile some find salvation in team-spirit and simple-minded solidarity, and some remain bereft. To survive at all they have to develop at least the illusion of a hefty carapace, to keep the painful feelings out and to keep the anger in. Disconcertingly the very ethos that has placed them in this mess contains the good old solid virtues that they need to master it, so that to add to their confusion it becomes impossible to distinguish where imposition

☞

"When I say I'm not the guy writing these songs, that's me squirming on the hook. On the other hand, I know what I meant at the time. As personal as these songs are—as much as I write about parents, wives, children, lovers—this job of writing songs, making CDs and doing shows comes down to a craft. It's a show. It's enhanced or souped up. My version of events is often quite true, but there has to be a beginning, a middle and an end. Her answer was that this argument was too pat, too facile. I might say that this is a version of me, not the real me, but that doesn't solve her problem, which is that I'm not around, and when I am, I'm uptight..."

ends and privilege begins.

Paradoxically Loudon's carapace consists of an almost arrogant truthfulness with which he unblinkingly describes his pain, gambling, as it were, that we have a similar pain but not the courage to confess it. You can imagine that he almost relishes our discomfort in hearing it. Someone else's pain, whether it's worse than yours or not as bad, is hard to bear. When it's described in stark simplicity it can even be embarrassing, and Loudon doesn't spare us that embarrassment. It goes against his instincts but does it anyway. He's not a rebel trying to shock us out of our complacency, he's a White Anglo Saxon Protestant, and he's embarrassed too. It's his own embarrassment he's working through, as well as ours. The irreconcilable ambivalence of his message, the ambivalence that keeps him behind his four foot wall is this: "This is how bad it is", he calmly states, as though hoping for our sympathy. But then he adds "You know what? I can take it. I can take it because that's the kind of guy I am." And we know what kind of guy he is: he's a one man guy. He doesn't need us.

There's a confusing contradiction here. On the one hand we recognise what is more or less an archetype of masculinity, the self-sufficient loner, riding out of town, but on the other we see that something's wrong. Where is the laconic taciturnity that is archetypal too? Few people have articulated with such clarity the workings of the primordial gulf between men and women. His subject matter, on the face of it intensely personal, is actually as universal and permanent as love itself, and it contains the fundamental conundrum at the heart of masculinity: we can't be loved until we let our defences down, and we'd be mad to let our defences down until we can be sure of love. In a catalogue of beautiful songs—"again and again about unhappy love, over and over, unhappy love"—he has minutely charted this dilemma, and all the circuitous stratagems with which we try to escape it. He says fame and wealth are what he's after, how he gets them he don't care. He goes out on the prowl, looking for an ingenue, he goes out on the road, trying just to get on with his job. But whatever it is he tries to do he always finds himself standing outside, looking on with sardonic detachment, unable to take the plunge. Fame and wealth are a well-known substitute, or perhaps a metaphor for love, and it would perhaps be truer to say that he has eluded them, rather than them eluding him. The right career moves in the early seventies, and once or twice since then, would have brought him fame and wealth, but it's plain that how he got them he *did* care, and he turned his back on them. For some reason much as he wants it he also despises it. He's a folk singer who laughs at folk, a country singer who mocks country, a would be megastar who despises megastars. Is there a touch of the Groucho Marxes here? If love were a club that was willing let him in, could it be good enough for him to want to join?

Where then do his fans fit into this ambivalence? What does he feel about them? What they lack in numbers they tend to make up for in unusual zeal. It's as though the fact that he isn't a big star, being swept away in long black limousines, enables them to feel that he's practically a mate. "Most fans are average guys and gals, anxious to be you bosom pals" he writes with characteristic gentle mockery in the wonderful but as yet unrecorded song My Biggest Fan. "My biggest fan is a 400 pound man", obviously dysfunctional then, but utterly dependable, benignly stalking him from gig to gig, he knows the words of all the songs better than Loudon does himself, and follows with obsessional interest the minutiae of his life. I feel sure I've met this man, and the other fans that are mentioned in the song. The intensity and industriousness with which Loudon's public follows him is intriguing and revealing. Perhaps it can be explained by a combination of the nature of the songs and his unusually purist working style. First there is the seeming indistinctness of the boundary between his life and art. The apparently artless self-revelation of his songs creates the illusion not just of a personal relationship, but of a personal relationship closer than you have with many of your friends. This illusion has further scope to flourish through his style of touring, travelling under his own steam, alone, from gig to gig, carrying his own guitar—"he's just like you and me!" You are quite liable to bump into him, just as you might bump into a friend. It's a strange, one-sided intimacy that seems to be all of a piece with the Gordian knot of maleness mentioned earlier. The Gordondon knot of maleness, we might call it in this case. Intimacy, that thing that men are said to dread, can in reality only

be a two-way thing, and the illusory one-way version creates uncomfortable distortions and crossed wires. "Some fans harrass and stalk" he says in My Biggest Fan, reminding us what a strange relationship it can be between a performer and his audience, and what an escalating cycle of neediness on their part and wariness on his can come from it. It's a cycle that in a different context isn't unfamiliar to most men. But then he turns the tables on himself; as in many of his songs there is a disarming twist in which he makes himself the fall-guy in the end. It turns out that even this his biggest fan, obsessive and devoted though he is, can only rank him third in the singer-songwriters' pantheon. "Hey I'm his Third Man, but he's still my biggest fan!"

This endearing and uncloying capacity for self-mockery is the principal ingredient in a humorous cocktail, which also contains a measure of spite and and one of bitterness, a couple of measures of ordinary good-natured incredulity at life, and a frosting of perservering cheerfulness, and is served on the house in generous quantities to wash down Loudon's work, which for all its apparent spontaneity is substantial, workmanlike and disciplined. On the face of it this doesn't solve the mystery with which we started out. It may sound just a bit utilitarian, but this is an artist who offers unequalled value for money in his work— entertainment, insight, wisdom, fun; surely the world would beat a path right to his door? But somehow, just like him, the world is holding back. Not sure quite what to make of him. Ambivalent. ❖

Loudon Goes Jazz!

By Douglas Hand

As we all know Loudon does sometimes like to avail us all of his wonderful voice without any musical accompaniment, but here was a very nice Christmas surprise.

I first heard it one Saturday night in December, while tuned into Charlie Gillett, (the Silver Fox, as he is sometimes known, discoverer of Dire Straits), on his very varied radio show on GLR, the BBC local radio station for London.

It was only announced as a special tune for Christmas by John Scofield on a Promo from Verve Records, and I must admit the name meant nothing to me. What a surprise was in store.

The track started very quietly, and soon turned out to be a very nice version of *The Little Drummer Boy*. Far removed from David Bowie/Bing Crosbie, it appeared to be a four piece band with a straight jazz interpretation, and some superb guitar work, until after about 2.50 into the track. Then a familiar voice appeared from the background—none other than the man himself, LWiii. The vocal is in a semi-spoken style at first until he gets more into it and opens up. I sat totally transfixed at this unexpected Christmas present, and revelled in it until it ended a minute or so later.

The production of the track was just amazing—so clear and sharp—especially since where I live the radio signal can be a little dubious at times. Would Charlie back-announce the track, and would I be able to get hold of it?

He did back-announce it after another tune—the wait seemed to be forever. It was a Christmas Promo from Verve Records, but it was only for the trade and some DJs and in very limited numbers.

I made several calls during the next few days to various record dealers but without success. Either they'd never seen it, or they'd had it but it had gone very quickly. There remained only one choice, a direct approach to the record label. After tracking them down it was not until after several calls that I was able to speak to someone, and of course I had no luck. As I was neither in the trade nor a DJ they wouldn't part with one of the few remaining copies no matter how I pleaded with them. I was resigned to failure and could only hope that a copy may turn up somewhere over the next few months.

Then—a letter from Kevin Harrison requesting material and suggestions for the revised version of this very book. But how could this help me?

One afternoon at work the answer hit me like a bolt from the blue. Here was the answer to my problem! But would it work?

Of course it did. Verve Records were only too pleased to send me a copy when I explained it was for an article in SMFS, and would receive fairly wide coverage.

So there we are, and here it is. The CD arrived nicely packaged in a special printed card slip cover. There was a semi-circle section cut out to reveal a spin game printed on the CD, which sat in a specially designed plastic tray. Another item for the LWiii collection, and a total delight to listen to as well. ❖

An American in PARiS

Caesar Glebbeek goes to see Loudon
for two concerts and an **interview**

On two hot days in the summer of 1999
Loudon was in Paris for two consecutive
gigs at the Hotel du Nord. Caesar
Glebbeek was there as well to record an
interview based on a set of questions
submitted by members of Ron Mura's
Internet discussion group, and he was
present at both shows.

The Hotel du Nord is an atmospheric
little venue on the banks of the Canal St.
Martin, a short green stretch of quiet
waterway a stone's throw from the Gare
de l'Est. In 1938 it was the setting for a
classic of French cinema, *Hotel du Nord,*
and its interior has recently been restored
to its 1930s decor; outside it retains an
unassuming look.

Loudon arrived in Paris at about 2 pm
and was met at the station by Karel Beer,
the promoter of the show, who took him
to the accommodation he'd undertaken to
provide—a tiny room without air-
conditioning in a small two-star hotel. At
around half past six Loudon arrived at
the venue for a soundcheck and some
photographs—for a forthcoming article in
the Herald Tribune it turned out. The
soundcheck was short, ten minutes at the
most. He played four songs including a
comically fast rendition of *One Man Guy,*
and then posed for the Herald Tribune
pictures before he went off to get a bite to
eat before the show. While he was away
attending to with the inner man the tables
around the tiny stage rapidly filled up
and the temperature steadily rose. As this
was France the room also steadily filled
with smoke. It was only slight compensa-
tion that many of the people puffing
away were very attractive ladies who had
decided to leave much of their clothing

Canal St Martin

off to celebrate the 31 degrees. Some of
them made it seem more like 45 degrees.

Shortly before nine o'clock Loudon
appeared on stage, and started the show
with *What Gives?* He followed with *One
Man Guy; Bridge; I'm Alright; Tonya's
Twirls; Inaugural Blues; Between; The
Picture* and with a wry reference to the
self-fumigating audience *New Street
People.* Then mopping himself with a
towel he said "This might cool us off a
bit" and sang *You Don't Want to Know.* It
didn't cool anybody off, but it's the
thought that counts. He went on to do
Unhappy Anniversary; Bed and *The Doctor*
before Karel Beer unexpectedly announced that there were to be two sets.
Loudon took this news in the unfazed
manner of someone used to dealing with

Loudon's-eye view, Hotel du Nord

a sudden change of plan, and told the audience he'd do one more song before the interval. He sang *Whatever Happened to Us* to close out the first half.

He opened the second half with *Natural Disaster*, followed by *Thank You Mr Hubble*, and *Conspiracies*. So far no one in the 200 strong audience had even murmured a request, so Caesar asked him if he'd do *Dreaming*. He said that was a little difficult—retuning was involved. "Something else then?" Caesar asked. "No, no, I'll do *Dreaming*", and he did. Then it was *Sleeping Around*, a very funny new one about all the places that boast "George Washington Slept Here", and then *The Man Who Couldn't Cry*, followed by *Rufus is a Tit Man, White Winos* and *Y2K* ("Don't forget to stock up on them freeze-dried croissants...!")

After this the promoter appeared again and said the man upstairs was complaining about the noise. The audience was told to be very quiet for the encore, which was fittingly *A Pretty Good Day So Far*.

After the show Loudon signed CDs and posters, and according to Yazid Manou, the PR man from Ryko who was there, 28 copies of *Social Studies* found new homes.

"I love Paris in the summer, when it sizzles" goes the song . The next day was hot again. Caesar's appointment for his interview was not till three in the afternoon so he took a stroll up to Montmartre and the Sacré Coeur where he could look at Paris laid out in the sun. On the way back later to his hotel he chanced to bump into Loudon who'd just been having lunch. He said he was tired, looking forward to his nap. In fact he'd like to keep the interview quite short— half an hour say. Caesar had been hoping for at least an hour, but there was nothing he could do. Loudon had a lot to do that afternoon. He had an interview at two o'clock, then Caesar, and five interviews by phone to Canada at half past four. Plus he had to get his nap.

Caesar turned up early, gambling correctly that the previous interview would also be for half an hour. During the interview Loudon seemed a little aloof, or perhaps just tired, at times, but he gave him forty minutes and some time for photographs. There wasn't time for all the questions on the list. What follows are edited highlights, rather than a live transmission of the match:

All Those Record Company Blues

CG: Would you be able to tell me why Virgin dropped you, or maybe you dropped Virgin?

LW: **Well, I think the reason that any record company decides to drop you or let you go is...**

CG: When the sales go down.

LW: **Yeah, I mean it's a business decision. So, I made four records for Virgin, and they're good records, and, er, they didn't make enough money to keep me I guess. So that's probably what happened.**

CG: And what's the situation now with Ryko? Do you have a multi-album deal with them?

LW: **I am contracted to make another record for them. It's a two-record deal. I don't know if it's a studio album. I don't know what it is, I haven't thought about what my next record's going to be.**

CG: Oh, I see. I thought you'd already made up your mind that it was going to be a studio release.

LW: **Well, I don't know. I can change my mind?**

CG: Yes, sure. But you have quite a few songs ready...

LW: **Oh, I know I have enough songs but I am not in any big rush. Why hurry? It could be a studio album, it could be a live album.**

CG: So there's no pressure to do anything at the moment?

LW: **No. In the new year, in the new millennium I'll think about the next record.**

CG: If we make it...

LW: **Right!**

Out on the Road

CG: Somebody wanted to know why you never had a roadie.

LW: **I'd have to pay him! I might have to break down and get a roadie as I am getting awfully tired of dragging this guitar around.**

CG: Do you actually make good money on the road?

LW: **Yeah, it's still a pretty good job. I mean, you know, I work hard but I can pay all the ex wives.**

CG: Is it still fun to go out on the road?

LW: **It's fun to play. It's not fun to travel. I love to play, it's exciting to write a new song, it's kind of interesting to try to make a new record, but the travel...**

CG: How do you prepare for a show?

LW: **I think about what I'm going to start with... You've seen enough shows to know that certain songs sometimes connect into other songs. But you know, it has a flow to it. I try to remember where I am and if there's a request that I want to do then I do it. If I don't want to do it, I won't do it. I don't really prepare, I mean, I drink a coffee, a lot of mineral water, I play the guitar and go out and sing.**

CG: But sometimes you come out with a piece of paper.

LW: **Sometimes I do, sometimes I don't, you know. Last night I just thought I would start with *What Gives?* and then, er, it moves, you know.**

CG: What about when you're done with a show, do you evaluate it?

LW: **Well, if I don't think I did a good**

☞

19

show I kick myself around a little bit. You like to do the best job you can do under the circumstances. Certain things are not under your control— if the sound isn't good, or the audiences…

CG: Drunken Scottish people in the crowd?

LW: Right! Ronnie Scott's.

The Heckler

CG: Are there any songs you wish people wouldn't request during the shows?

LW: Well I go through period when I am tired of certain songs. I mean, one of the songs that's popular is *The Acid Song* and I'm in the point now where I may want to do it next year, but I am tired of doing it. I mean I might do it tonight, too, but when I hear that [request] I just kinda go, 'Nah!'

CG: Do you get disturbed by say over-boisterous people at your shows?

LW: No, because I like to make them laugh. I enjoy that…

CG: But at Ronnie Scott's you gave the girl the 2-minute warning there.

LW: Right. Well, sometimes people cross the line, you know, and you deal with that. The problem with that is that you don't want to attack those people, but they were ruining the show for other people. So, real life intrudes.

CG: Well, I thought if it gets too much, those people should be removed from the venue.

LW: Yeah, that would have been a good thing if somebody had come up to them and given them the two-minute warning, and said, 'If we have to come up again, you'll have to leave.'

Caesar Glebbeek, Loudon and André Van den Berg outside the Hotel du Nord

CG: Because they are actually spoiling it for the other 150 people there...

LW: Yeah, yeah. Anyway, we survived!

Don't Do Stuff You Don't want to Do... So Pardon Me But ... No!

CG: Back in 1992, Richard Thompson gave a series of so-called "request only" shows at "The Bottom Line" in New York City. Basically what happened was that people came into the venue and wrote single requests on a piece of paper and dropped them into a bucket on stage. Then Rich would play whatever came out of the bucket; the shows were absolutely hilarious. Would you ever consider doing such a show?

LW: **Well, I like to have a little more control over things... I'm not going to do it!**

CG: Too much hassle?

LW: **I don't need to do it. I've got an agenda. When I walk onto a stage I want to get certain things down. I am happy to take requests from the floor...**

CG: Well, it would be a one-off...

LW: *(slightly irritated)* **Why? I don't need a gimmick. I can't waste a night doing that, I gotta get the word out there.**

CG: Okay. Well, Richard doesn't do it anymore. This was way, way back in time.

LW: *(laughing)* **Yeah! It was such a great idea, he doesn't do it anymore! Now you want *me* to do it!**

CG: Well, I just thought it was a nice idea, you know.

LW: **Right, right. Why don't *you* do it?!**

The Home Stretch

CG: Now when you're touring do you look forward to going home again?

LW: **You mean stop touring and start resting? Yeah, I'm dying to go home and rest.**

CG: You once said you would stop playing at the age of 50. You are still at it...

LW: **When did I say that? I'm going to retire when I'm 75 now. We move it up! If Clark Terry can be playing when he's 78 years old I can go to 75.**

What Are Families For?

CG: *What Are Families For?*—How did you get the idea for that song?

LW: **The difficulty of dealing with your family, dealing with your brothers and sisters even after you've all grown up. Somehow you assume that when you get to be twenty years old that all the problems that you've had as kids, you know sibling rivalry... and my experience is that is just gets worse. So I think that's what inspired that song. You know, the idea of "When I was a kid I used to push my baby brother's face into the ground..." And that kind of cruelty that children have to each other, it creates a kind of, er... It's almost like the Balkan situation, you know—the legacy of violence in the family just festers and gets worse and worse and worse. So the next thing is, you try to deal with each other and you're fifty years old, and all those resentments are still there. I think that's what that song is about.**

☞

21

And the dynamic, the power of the parents, and being in the car... and that whole thing.

CG: You haven't played it for a while actually.

LW: No, it's a hard song to do. It's a good song but it takes a really special quiet theme from the audience to get across. It's also quite funny. It can be.

My Strong Buddies

CG: What about taking some people with you on the road—is it uneconomical?

LW: Yeah, well, there's an economic situation. I don't know that my fans really require that, you know. They kind of like to see me solo anyway. But if I could afford it I'd probably bring David Mansfield, Chaim Tannenbaum, and this new bass player I've got, Greg Cohen. But you know, these guys are expensive and they are busy. Chaim Tannenbaum is a schoolteacher—a college professor—so he's teaching for a lot of the year, too. So he's not [always] available.

Absence Makes the Heart Grow Fonder

CG: Somebody wanted me to ask you about your comfort level when playing with the McGarrigles. He saw you in Minnesota and...

LW: *(laughing)* And I seemed tense?

CG: A little tense.

LW: Minnesota. That was a good show. I was good, I remember... I like singing with the McGarrigles.

Oh Muse Where Are You

CG: Lets move to songwriting now. Where does you appetite for sarcasm comes from? From your dad? Or maybe I should say witty...

LW: I don't know if that could be traced to either parent or both parents.

CG: Was your father a funny man?

LW: Oh, he was a very funny man, but I wouldn't describe him as being sarcastic...

CG: But you have a tendency sometimes to be a *little bit* sarcastic at times.

LW: Oh, yeah, but I don't know where that comes from.

CG: What comes first, the lyrics or the music?

LW: Generally the lyrics.

CG: Do you discipline yourself to write a certain amount every day or week?

LW: No, I don't have anything that's... If a certain amount of time goes by and I haven't written anything I get nervous.

CG: Do you still have a creative need to write songs?

LW: Well, it's my job.

CG: And do you have lots of half-finished songs?

LW: I have songs that I've thrown out...

CG: Do you completely throw them out?

LW: No, sometimes I dig them up and use a line or half a verse.

CG: Do you keep a notebook?

LW: I have a lot of notebooks which I am gonna *burn* before I die...

Daddy Takes a Nap

CG: Now...

LW: **We're in the home stretch right here?**

CG: Oh, goodness me, are we?

LW: **Quick, quick, quick, as I want to lie down!**

CG: Goodness me, he needs his nap! Eh, your popularity, or sometimes lack of it, is there any single reason for it?

LW: **It's not my concern. My job is to write the songs, do the best shows I can, make the best records I can, do the nicest interviews I can. And get my ass from A to B. That's my job. Whether I'm popular in this place is not my concern.**

CG: What's your biggest hobby after music?

LW: **Napping!**

CG: Napping, right. Seriously *(Loudon making snoring noises)*, have you got any hobbies?

LW: **Nap time. No, no hobbies, I like to nap and...**

CG: So what do you do when you're at home then?

LW: **Wait for the phone to ring.**

CG: Another gig?

LW: **Another woman!**

CG: Now, eh...

LW: **You got two more minutes, Caesar!**

CG: Goodness me! You are familiar with *Desert Island*, the concept?

LW: ***Desert Island Discs*? Yeah.**

CG: If you were asked to go there, what would you take along?

LW: **Sunblock!**

CG: What's the weirdest thing you have heard or read about yourself?

LW: **That I was the "male Melanie."**

LW: **Last question!**

CG: Alright—anything to declare?

LW: **Er... [Long pause] No!**

CG: Okay. Thank you!

LW: **Thank you... See you later.**

The audience for the second concert was smaller than the night before. 150, possibly. When Karel Beer introduced the show he had a solution to the environmental problems of the night before: he asked if the audience would smoke as little as possible, and compensate by drinking more.

The Future!

Photo: Philip Boxall

Loudon came on and shared with the audience some of the disgusting sights he'd seen in Paris as he'd walked about that day—people kissing each other everywhere you turn, and holding hands—before he opened up with *People in Love*, followed by *So Many Songs*.

Right at the front there was a family group including two young boys. Loudon asked one of them how old he was.

"Seven".

"Are You a Fan?"

"Oh Yes."

"The future!" Loudon proclaimed, turning to the audience. He asked the youngster if he had a favourite song, but he couldn't think of one straight off, so Loudon spent a few minutes plugging *Social Studies*, reminding the audience that copies were on sale at the show. Not only would he sign them, he'd even lick them if they liked!

Then he did *What Gives, New Street People* and *Plane Too*. By this time the boy had chosen his request, *Human Cannon-ball*, which Loudon followed with *Between, Bein' a Dad, Homeless, White Winos* and *The Home Stretch* and took a well earned break.

The first song of the second half was *When I'm at Your House* and then came *Five Years Old*. There was some banter with a French fan whom Loudon seemed to know from a previous appearance at the Hotel du Nord. Then the French fan shouted "Loudon, are you all right?" which was the cue for *I'm Alright*. Then *Inaugural Blues, Bad Man* and *Carmine Street*. In the next song, *Motel Blues* he turned to his youngest fans after the line 'Sleep with Me' explaining "It's like a pyjama party kids".

Motel Blues 2 followed (aka *Wires in the Rug*), and then *Bed; Living Alone; I Walked Through the Graveyard; Y2K; Summer's Almost Over; Men* (very popular with this audience) and *Tip That Waitress*. For an encore there was *Pretty Good Day So Far* and *A Song*. It was a marvellous show.

The usual selling, signing, licking session afterwards, and everyone went their separate ways into the balmy Paris night.

The next day Loudon got up and went for a relaxing morning stroll before, suitcase and guitar in hand, he took the Eurostar to England and an unusual engagement on the John Peel show, broadcast late at night and live from the DJ's rural home.

Do you have a preference for being classified as folk, or pop, rock? Does it matter? I mean, when they stick you into the folks section, would it be better to have you in the rock section, you know?
"It doesn't matter really. They should stick me in the classical section! Polka!"

CG/SMFS

Home Team Crowd

Some Reflections from Fans

THE SINGING LIZINGO

History was the first Loudon Wainwright album I bought. Kinda sadly the motivation behind my purchase was a little tentative. I had heard that my idol, American recording artist Steve Forbert, was mentioned in the lyric of one of the songs on this album. My thinking was that anyone cool enough to name-check Steve deserved to be listened to too and I'm glad I did. I have subsequently been exposed to so many fabulous songs: *Tip That Waitress*, *Grown Man* and *Primrose Hill* to name just three. Of course back then I had 22 years and 12 previous albums of LW3 history to check out.

> ".. Yeah, I got a deal and so did John Prine,
> Steve Forbert and Springsteen all in a line.
> They were lookin for you, signin' up others. We were new Bob Dylans ... "
> Talkin' New Bob Dylan (1992)

In July 1996 at the Barbican Centre in London I saw Loudon in concert for the first time. Magic and melody filled the warm summer air that night as the 49 year old 'new Bob Dylan' on stage strummed his guitar sang his often thought provoking and witty short stories, while he spasmodically poked out his tongue and periodically raised and lowered a leg. It occurred to me, just briefly, that Loudon could be likened to a lizard on stage on account of his darting tongue, or even a flamingo because of his one-legged stances. A singing lizingo, or maybe a minstrel flamand. But that sounds more like a chocolate dessert than a talented entertainer of the highest order

In October 1997 I was lucky enough to talk briefly to Loudon at The Borderline in London. We had both gone along to see the singer-songwriter performing there that night, a 42 year old 'new Bob Dylan' from Meridian Mississippi named Steve Forbert. In truth our conversation was a little one sided: I blurted out *"Hello Loudon, I am coming to see you later this month at the Union Chapel in Islington, I am really, looking forward to it. I like the new album. especially 'Bein' a Dad' nice to meet you, goodbye. "* Loudon smiled sweetly during my verbal onslaught, but I could tell he was probably thinking: Who is this idiot? Leave me alone I am trying to listen to my friend Steve'.

Michael Herbert

LOUDON WAINWRIGHT AT THE PLACE, CHICAGO

I am used to seeing Loudon in large venues, such as the London Dominion, or The Paladium so it came as a surprise to find our man performing at a smallish musical venue in Chicago back in '93.

I arrived early with a friend who knew very little about Loudon, despite being very knowledgeable about rock music in general. We sipped drinks at a table near the front of the stage and I chatted with a couple of Loudon fans who had frequently seen him at The Place. They told me that Loudon had often performed at this venue and in the past had performed two or even three sets. The best one being the last when he was not so sober and sang his more risqué material.

Loudon duly performed in his customary manner; always thoroughly professional, sometimes playing the braggart, sometimes apparently lovelorn, sensitive, then suddenly brash again, swatting hecklers with ease. In fact this was a peak period for Loudon. He had been on prestigious national radio in mid-week discussing his 'mid life crisis' or 'divorce' songs. The interviewer asked him which classic song he wished he had written and as a response he sang My Girl.

At The Place I watched him perform *He Said, She Said* for the first time. The wonderful thing about Loudon is that he can write a great song at any given time. So many songwriters run out of inspiration after the first couple of albums. Not so Loudon. He is a man for all seasons. In fact he proved this point on this occasion. I recall the event was staged around Halloween, so Loudon duly included a Halloween song plus his Vampire song. He dryly noted that as usual the Christmas sales had started in October, so he sang a song satirising the very long Christmas season everyone had to endure.

I returned home blissful. My friend was in disbelief that someone as good as Loudon Wainwright had been a mystery to him until that evening. It is odd that Loudon is a bigger star in London than in Chicago. I guess the prophet has to go overseas to be recognised.

Richard Kemble

Home Team Crowd

Some Reflections from Fans

LOUDO'S COLUMBIA YEARS: AN APPRECIATION

With the recent reissue of two Loudon Wainwright albums on the Columbia label from the early 1970s on CD, the time seems right for a reassessment of a brief, but much-maligned period in his recording career.

Loudon has personally contributed to the critical tendency to downgrade the Columbia albums because of problems he encountered in 1972-74 with alleged production shortcomings, management hassles and the mounting pressure to produce another big hit single on the scale of Dead Skunk." But as DH Lawrence said in 1923: "Never trust the artist — trust the tale."

I believe the best of the Columbia years can easily stand comparison with the finest work Loudon has produced as a mature, label-hopping artist.

Ironically, although it contained the huge single, "Dead Skunk," Loudon's first album for Columbia, 1972's Album III, was his weakest. Despite the razor-sharp social commentary of "Drinking Song" and the positively psychotic "Muse Blues," much of the album was lacklustre, and a cover of Leiber and Stoller's "Smokey Joe's Café" was surely premature for an aspiring singer-songwriter.

But the following year's "Attempted Mustache" was indisputably the real thing. Despite criticism aimed by Loudon at Bob Dylan's famed producer, Bob Johnston, I believe the album is a high watermark in his early career.

The songs possess an edgy, fired-up, off-the-wall quality often ironed out in the mature albums. "Swimming Song," the opener, is the buoyant great hit single that never was; "Clockwork Chartreuse" and "Nocturnal Stumblebutt," a strange amalgam of George Jones and William Burroughs; while perfect cameos like "Liza" are complemented by the bleak emotionalism of "Lullaby." And we mustn't forget a major Wainwright song in "The Man Who Couldn't Cry" and the fabulous support of illustrious Nashville Cats such as Kenneth Buttrey, Mac Gayden and Reggie Young.

The cracks in Loudon's increasingly fraught relationship with Columbia were beginning to show by the time of the "Unrequited" album in 1975. The split between the studio tracks and the live recordings from The Bottom Line in Loudon's native New York City revealed the almost schizophrenic nature of both the singer and his label's plans for his career strategy. Still, the studio cuts included gems like "Absence Makes the Heart Grow Fonder" and the starkly beautiful "Kick in the Head."

But the real gold on "Unrequited" is contained in The Bottom Line tracks, which remain Loudon's finest live recordings. Artist and audience seem joined at the hip in terms of intimate rapport, with "Hardy Boys at the Y," the revisited bleakness of "Old Friend," the chirpy "Guru" and the singalong "Unrequited to the Nth Degree" being perfect examples of Loudon Wainwright's brilliant stagecraft.

Terry Kelly

OLYMPIA THEATRE, DUBLIN

I must have been crazy! I had nowhere to stay that night in Dublin because every hotel and guest house had been booked up for almost the past six weeks, (special holiday weekend), and I had only found out about the Dublin concert two weeks before. I sometimes think, and I'm sure a lot of readers would agree with me, that LWiii concert dates are closely-guarded secrets, and unless you happen to pick up the right magazine or paper at the right time Loudon can pop in and play a concert without you being aware of it. I only found out about the current tour by picking up a discarded copy of *Q* magazine on an underground train while on a visit to London. It didn't mention the Irish concert though. I found out about that from the *Rosebud* website. Incidentally the *Virgin* website (Loudon's record label in Britain at the time) didn't help much: they informed me that he was currently not on tour!

So off I went on the 100 mile, 3 hour trip to Dublin. I hadn't even got a ticket—*HMV* ticketshop wouldn't book one by credit card because it was too close to the concert itself—so I just had to go down and take a chance there'd be some left. All they had was one in the back row of the circle, or some in the third row of the gallery! I had a phone number of someone I might have been able to stay with overnight, but he worked on a newspaper and was rarely in. I could have been lucky. As it turned out I wasn't, but that's the story of my life!

What about the gig? Well there was no David Mansfield, and not even Peter Blegvad. There was, however, a support band called *Naked*, apparently an 'upcoming Dublin band'. (Well that's what it said on the printed cards that were dotted around the bar.) There was a personal message from them too, thanking Loudon for this opportunity of supporting him, and yes, believe it or not, they spelt his name 'with an *e* between the *d* and the *n*', as in TSMNWA. Nearly as bad as the actual ticket agency, who had him listed on their computer as London Wainwright! What were *Naked* like on stage? Well they were sort of as good as Boo Hewardine, if that means anything. After two numbers I just had to get back to the bar, only returning when the man himself came out.

Never mind 'a spiral notebook and a Scripto pencil'—all I had was a Bic biro, the envelope that came with my ticket and the back of a handbill for a new pizza restaurant that someone handed me outside the theatre. Believe me it's extremely difficult to jot down notes on a piece of paper on your knee, especially when you're having to write in total darkness . . .

Martin Maguire

Index of Songs

LWiii credits this song to Marty Robbins, John Peel Show 29/7/99

30

Index of Songs

Index of Songs

Index of Songs

Index of Songs

Index of Songs

[1] *This Song Don't Have a Video*
[2] *They Spelt My Name Wrong Again*

Index of Songs

Glasgow 30 May 1998

"I know a few chords. I can play the guitar, I've got a good right hand. But I'm not working on my musical development. I'm not taking guitar lessons or anything" (TJ/S: 31/7/76)

The Albums

Loudon Wainwright III   1970
Produced by LWIII and Milton Kramer
LP: Atlantic SD 8260 (US)
LP: Atlantic 2400 103 (UK)
LP: Edsel (1989 re-release)

1	Schooldays	3.04
2	Hospital Lady	4.03
3	Ode to Pittsburgh	3.13
4	Glad to See You've Got Religion	3.53
5	Uptown	2.42
6	Black Uncle Remus	2.37
7	Four Is a Magic Number	3.26
8	I Don't Care	4.07
9	Central Square Song	526
10	Movies Are a Mother to Me	2.36
11	Bruno's Place	3.31

Album II   1971
Produced by LWIII and Milton Kramer
LP: Atlantic SD 8291 (US)
LP: Atlantic K40272 (UK)
LP: Edsel ED310 (1989 re-release)

1	Me and My Friend the Cat	3.16
2	Motel Blues	2.43
3	Nice Jewish Girls	2.02
4	Be Careful,There's a Baby in the House	3.17
5	I Know I'm Unhappy/	
	Suicide Song/Glenville Reel	3.03
6	Saw Your Name in The Paper	2.07
7	Samson and the Warden	2.59
8	Plane; Too	3.05
9	Cook That Dinner, Dora	2.00
10	Old Friend	2.52
11	Old Paint (Traditional)	3.46
12	Winter Song	3.26

Album III (with White Cloud)   1972
Produced by Thomas Jefferson Kaye Kramer
LP: Columbia KC 31462 (US)
LP: CBS 65238 (UK)
CD: CK31462

1	Dead Skunk	3.08
2	Red Guitar	1.47
3	East Indian Princess	2.57
4	Muse Blues	2.55
5	Hometeam Crowd	1.50
6	B Side	2.27
7	Needless To Say	3.13
8	Smokey Joe's Cafe	
	(Jerry Leiber and Mike Stoller)	2.31
9	New Paint	3.02
10	Trilogy (Circa 1967)	3.12
11	Drinking Song	2.54
12	Say That You Love Me	2.29

Attempted Mustache   1973
Produced by Bob Johnston
LP: Columbia KC 32710 (US)
LP: CBS 65837 (UK)
CD: Edsel EDCD269
CD: Columbia CK65257 (1998)

1	The Swimming Song	2.26
2	A.M. World	2.31
3	Bellbottom Pants	2.27
4	Liza	2.47
5	I am the Way	
	(W. Guthrie, new lyrics by LWiii)	3.12
6	Clockwork Chartreuse	3.37
7	Down Drinking at the Bar	3.55
8	The Man Who Couldn't Cry	6.16
9	Come a Long Way (Kate McGarrigle)	2.45
10	Nocturnal Stumblebutt	3.45
11	Dilated to meet You	2.02
12	Lullaby	2.55

The Albums

Album III
1972

Unrequited · 1975
Produced by LWIII
LP: Columbia PC 33369 (US)
LP: CBS 80696 (UK)
CD: Edsel EDCD273 (1988)
CD: Columbia/Legacy CK 65258 (1998)

1	Sweet Nothings	2.46
2	Lowly Tourist, The	3.28
3	Kings and Queens	
	(*LWIII & George Gerdes*)	2.21
4	Kick in the Head	2.49
5	Whatever Happened to Us?	2.05
6	Crime of Passion	2.57
7	Absence Makes the Heart Grow Fonder	3.06
8	On the Rocks	2.45
9	Guru	2.08
10	Mr Guilty	3.15
11	The Hardy Boys at the Y*	2.56
12	Unrequited to the Nth Degree	2.48
13	Old Friend	2.38
14	Rufus is a Tit Man	1.44

1998 CD CK65258 contains the following extra tracks:
15. Rufus Is a Tit Man alternative version
16. Over the Hill (*LWiii and Kate McGarrigle*)
17. Hollywood Hopeful alternative version

*Appeared as Untitled on US albums because of legal problems over name "Hardy Boys" by F. W. Dixon

"...This brought a brief glimpse of the big time— getting picked up in limousines to go and judge skunk contests..." (BT/IoS 27/9/92)

T Shirt · 1976
Produced by LWIII
LP: Arista AL4063 (US)
LP: Arista ARTY127 (UK)

1. Bicentennial
2. Summer's Almost Over
3. Hollywood Hopeful
   (*Words LWIII, Music Trad Folk Song "Little Sadie"*)
4. Reciprocity
5. At Both Ends
6. Wine With Dinner
7. Hey Packy (*George Gerdes*)
8. California Prison Blues
9. Talking Big Apple '75
10. Prince Hal's Dirge
11. Just Like President Thieu
12. Wine with Dinner (Night Cap)

Final Exam (with Slow Train) · 1978
Produced by John Lissauer
LP: Arista AB4173 (US)
LP: Arista SPART1042 (UK)
LP: Poopik Productions AB4173 (Europe)

1	Final Exam	3.46
2	Mr Guilty	4.20
3	Penpal Blues	2.57
4	Golfin' Blues	?2.5
5	Heckler, The	4.25
6	Natural Disaster	3.45
7	Fear with Flying	3.41
8	Heaven and Mud	2.49
9	Two-song Set	3.35
10	Pretty Little Martha	2.58
11	Watch Me Rock, I'm Over thirty	2.49

I'm Alright
1985

The Albums

A Live One   1979
Produced by John Wood and LWiii
LP: Rounder 3050 (US)
LP: Radar RAD24 (UK)
CD: Edsel EDCD223

1	Motel Blues	3.41
2	Hollywood Hopeful*	1.25
3	Whatever Happened to Us?	1.56
4	Natural Disaster	2.21
5	Suicide Song	2.27
6	School Days	3.33
7	Kings and Queens	2.42
8	Down Drinking at the Bar	4.05
9	B-Side	2.21
10	Nocturnal Stumblebutt	3.58
11	Red Guitar	1.57
12	Clockwork Chartreuse	4.13
13	Lullaby	3.02

Fame and Wealth   1983
Produced by LWiii
LP: Rounder 3076 (US)
LP: Demon FIEND5 (UK)

1	Reader and Advisor	5.17
2	Grammy Song, The	2.32
3	Dump the Dog	2.01
4	Thick and Thin	2.39
5	Revenge	2.36
6	Five Years Old	3.08
7	Ingenue	3.31
8	I.D.T.T.Y.W.L.M.*	4.01
9	Westchester County	2.46
10	Saturday Morning Fever	2.12
11	April Fool's Day Morn	4.20
12	Fame and Wealth	1.30

I'm Alright   1985
Produced by Richard Thompson and LWiii
LP: Rounder 3096 (US)
LP: Demon FIEND54 (UK)
CD: Rounder 3096

1	One Man Guy	4.11
2	Lost Love	3.19
3	I'm Alright	2.20
4	Not John	4.20
5	Cardboard Boxes	3.07
6	Screaming Issue (*LWiii and Terre Roche*)	4.47
7	How Old Are You?	2.09
8	Animal Song	2.11
9	Out of This World	3.13
10	Daddy, Take a Nap	3.55
11	Ready or Not (So Ripe)	4.13
12	Career Moves	3.15

The Albums

Therapy
1989

More Love Songs — 1986

Produced by Richard Thompson, LWiii
and Chaim Tannenbaum
LP: Rounder 3106 (US)
LP: Demon FIEND 79 (UK)
CD: Rounder 3106
CD: Demon FIEND 79 (UK)

1   Hard Day on the Planet
2   Synchronicity
3   Your Mother and I
4   I Eat Out
5   No
6   The Home Stretch
7   Unhappy Anniversary
8   Man's World
9   Vampire Blues
10 Overseas Call
11 Expatriot
12 The Back Nine   Extra track (7) on CD, The Acid Song

Therapy — 1989

Produced by Chaim Tannenbaum and LWiii
LP: Silvertone 1203-1-J
LP: Silvertone ORE LP 500
CD: Silvertone ORE CD 500

1	Therapy	4.19
2	Bill of Goods	3.15
3	T.S.D.H.A.V.*	2.05
4	Harry's Wall	5.19
5	Aphrodisiac	3.43
6	Fly Paper	4.08
7	Nice Guys	2.58
8	Thanksgiving	5.36
9	Your Father's Car	2.21
10	Me and All the Other Mothers	3.00
11	You Don't Want to Know	3.43
12	Mind Read (It Belonged to You)	2.42
13	This Year	3.02

Fame and Wealth / I'm Alright — 1991

CD Demon FIEND 711 (UK)

Contains all the songs on Fame and Wealth
(1983) and I'm Alright (1985) except
'Revenge' and 'Out of this World'

History — 1992

Produced by LWiii and Jeffrey Lesser
CD: Virgin/Charisma V2-86416 (US)
CD: Virgin CDV2703 (UK and Europe)

1	People in Love	2.59
2	Men	3.36
3	The Picture	2.32
4	When I'm at Your House	2.31
5	The Doctor	4.01
6	Hitting You	3.04
7	I'd Rather Be Lonely	2.50
8	Between	1.27
9	Talking New Bob Dylan	3.35
10	So Many Songs	3.53
11	4x10	3.06
12	A Father and a Son	3.20
13	Sometimes I Forget	4.52
14	Handful of Dust (*LW jnr*)	3.24

"I'm back where I grew up in
Westchester County...All the
guys take the train to the city
every day; I go in a couple of
times to see my shrink...
When he's cured me I can say
'Look this is what
I was like before!'"

History
1992

Career Moves   1993
Produced by LWiii and Jeffrey Lesser
CD: Virgin CDV2718

1	Road Ode	5.09
2	I'm Alright	2.59
3	Five Years Old	3.08
4	Your Mother and I	2.29
5	Westchester County	3.20
6	He said, She said	3.30
6.1	*Christmas Rap (Spoken)*	0.26
7	Suddenly It's Christmas	2.23
8	Thanksgiving	4.50
8.1	*A Fine Celtic Name, (Spoken)*	2.56
9	T.S.M.N.W.A.*	3.28
9.1	*Some Balding Guys (Spoken)*	1.27
10	The Swimming Song	2.25
11	Absence Makes the Heart Grow Fonder	3.00
12	Happy Birthday, Elvis	2.46
12.1	*Fabulous Songs (Spoken)*	0.26
13	Unhappy Anniversary	2.54
14	I'd Rather Be Lonely	2.58
14.1	*Just Say No (Spoken)*	0.33
15	April Fool's Day Morn	4.12
16	The Man Who Couldn't Cry	5.05
17	The Acid Song	5.54
18	Tip That Waitress	4.15
19	Career Moves	3.00

**I am a natural performer.
When I was seven I discovered
that I liked showing off. When
there's 2000 people in the
dark watching and the lights
are all on you, I find that
delightful**

Photo: Linda Haslett ©

One Man Guy: 1994
The Best Of Loudon Wainwright III
1982-1986
Produced by Richard Thompson,
LWiii, Chaim Tannenbaum
CD: Music Club MCCD 166

1	Hard Day on the Planet
2	Your Mother and I
3	Reader and Advisor
4	Cardboard Boxes
5	One Man Guy
6	I Eat Out
7	Thick and Thin (CD labelled incorrectly states 'Five Years Old')
8	Westchester County
9	I'm Alright
10	Not John
11	How Old Are You?
12	Acid Song, The
13	Dump the Dog
14	Career Moves
15	Fame and Wealth
16	Grammy Song, The
17	IDTTYWLM*
18	Ready Or Not (So Ripe)
19	Synchronicity
20	Lost Love
21	Unhappy Anniversary

The Albums

Grown Man
1995

Grown Man   1995
Produced by Jeffrey Lesser and LWiii
CD: Virgin CDV2789

1	The Birthday Present	1.52
2	Grown Man	3.51
3	That Hospital	3.58
4	Housework	4.39
5	Cobwebs	3.09
6	A Year	3.55
7	Father/Daughter Dialogue	2.35
8	1994	3.29
9	I.W.I.W.A.L*	3.06
10	Just A John	4.15
11	I Suppose	2.24
12	Dreaming	3.12
13	The End Has Begun	4.00
14	Human Cannonball	3.05
15	Treasure Untold (*Jimmie Rodgers*)	2.17

Little Ship   1997
Produced by John Leventhall and LWiii
CD:Virgin CDV 2644

1	Breakfast in Bed	3.05
2	Four Mirrors	2.55
3	Mr Ambivalent	3.44
4	OGM	2.55
5	Our Own War	3.50
6	So Damn Happy	2.25
7	Primrose Hill	4.47
8	Underwear	1.30
9	World, The	1.49
10	What Are Families For?	4.26
11	Bein' A Dad	3.41
12	Birthday Present ii, The	3.51
13	I Can't Stand Myself	3.41
14	Little Ship	3.35
15	A Song	3.05

The BBC Sessions   1998
CD: Strange Fruit SFRS CD073

1	Be Careful There's a Baby in the House (18/5/71)	3.19
2	East Indian Princess (18/5/71)	2.36
3	I Know I'm Unhappy/Suicide Song/ Grenville Reel (18/5/71)	3.21
4	A.M. World (11/6/73)	2.05
5	The Swimming Song (9/8/76)	2.53
6	Prince Hal's Dirge (9/8/76)	3.39
7	I Wish It Was Me (17/9/85)	1.25
8	No (17/9/85)	3.30
9	Hard Day on the Planet (17/9/85)	4.22
10	You Don't Want to Know (13/8/87)	4.13
11	Sunday Times (8/10/89)	2.47
12	Nice Guys (13/10/89)	2.47
13	Harry's Wall (13/10/89)	4.56
14	Carmine Street (1/10/92)	2.49
15	Number One (1/10/92)	3.41
16	The Birthday Present (ii) (1/10/92)	1.38
17	Men (26/9/92)	3.19
18	A Father and a Son (26/9/92)	3.07
19	School Days (26/9/92)	3.13
20	It's Love and I Hate It (14/8/93)	2.12
21	One Man Guy (14/8/93)	4.11

Photo Caesar Glebbeck ©

BBC Sessions
1998

Social Studies 1999

Produced by:
CD: Hannibal HNCD 1442

1	What Gives	3.30
2	Tonya's Twirls	3.38
3	New Street People	2.50
4	Carmine Street	2.58
5	O. J.	3.15
6	Leap of Faith	2.53
7	Conspiracies	2.17
8	Christmas Morning	3.36
9	Y2K	6.12
10	Number One	3.43
11	Bad Man	3.20
12	Inaugural Blues	3.18
13	Our Boy Bill	3.10
14	Jesse Don't Like It	4.08
15	Pretty Good Day	4.23

Photo: Linda Haslett/Darren

Schuba's, Chicago April 1998

"How Old Are You" is Loudon's anti-interview song. Having just arrived in Ireland a jet-lagged LWiii went through one such gruelling interview, live on radio, with an interviewer he later described as "not having a clue", and who for 20 minutes asked such pertinent questions as "Are you a sex symbol?" Finally Loudon was asked "what musicians do you look up to?" Loudon answered: "Well, I like David Byrne, have you heard of him?" ... "No" "He's a musician. Have you heard of Tom Petty?" ... "No" "He's a musician. Have you heard of Englebert Humperdink? ..."Yes" "Well I don't look up to him at all!" RO'D /MMM

Singles and Samplers

1994
VIRGIN CDVDJ 2789 PROMO CD 4 TRACK SAMPLER

Bellbottom Pants
CBS

Bicentennial
Talkin' Big Apple (B side)
ARISTA 53 US WHITE LABEL PROMO 7"

Cardboard Boxes
Colours (B side)
DEMON D1039 STOCK UK 7" ISSUE

Cobwebs
VIRGIN CDVDJ 2789 PROMO CD 4 TRACK SAMPLER

Dead Skunk
Needless to Say (B side)
CBS 1120 UK WHITE LABEL PROMO 7"

COLUMBIA 4-457626 Stock US 7" issue
Down Drinking at the Bar
I am the Way (B side)
CBS 2172 7" SINGLE

Dreaming
VIRGIN CDVDJ 2789 PROMO CD 4 TRACK SAMPLER

End Has Begun, The
VIRGIN CDVDJ 2789 PROMO CD 4 TRACK SAMPLER

Father/Daughter Dialogue
VIRGIN CDVDJ 2789 PROMO CD 4 TRACK SAMPLER

Five Years Old
Rumbunctious (B side)
DEMON D1016 UK PICTURE SLEEVE 7"

Grown Man
VIRGIN CDVDJ 2789 PROMO CD 4 TRACK SAMPLER

Housework
VIRGIN CDVDJ 2789 PROMO CD 4 TRACK SAMPLER

Human Cannonball
VIRGIN CDVDJ 2789 PROMO CD 4 TRACK SAMPLER

I Suppose
VIRGIN CDVDJ 2789 PROMO CD 4 TRACK SAMPLER

I.W.I.W.A.L[1]
VIRGIN CDVDJ 2789 PROMO CD 4 TRACK SAMPLER

Jesse Don't Like It
TSDHAV[2] B side
HANNIBAL HNC 0705 UK PICTURE SLEEVE 7"
HANNIBAL HNS 0705 US PICTURE SLEEVE 7"

Just A John
VIRGIN CDVDJ 2789 PROMO CD 4 TRACK SAMPLER

Mr Ambivalent
VIRGIN LOUDCDJ97, LC3098 ONE TRACK PROMO
MY GIRL
DEMON D1050 UK PICTURE SLEEVE 7"

People in Love
CHARISMA 12764 CANADIAN PROMO

Suddenly It's Christmas
VIRGIN BIGLDJ1 PROMO 1 TRACK CD

T.S.D.H.A.V.[2]
Nice Guys (B side)
SILVERSTONE ORE 15 UK PICTURE SLEEVE 7"

Talking New Bob Dylan
VIRGIN LWCDJ2 PROMO 1 TRACK CD

Thanksgiving
SILVERTONE RECORDS CD SAMPLER 1990 TD74540

This Year
SILVERTONE ONE SIDE PROMO 7" PICTURE
SLEEVE

Treasure Untold
VIRGIN CDVDJ 2789 PROMO CD 4 TRACK SAMPLER

Unhappy Anniversary
Acid Song (B side)
DEMON D1044 STOCK UK 7" ISSUE

Y2K
HANNIBAL PROMO SINGLE 1999 (3 VERSIONS)

Year, A
VIRGIN CDVDJ 2789 PROMO CD 4 TRACK
SAMPLER

Your Mother and I
End of a Long Lonely Day (B side)
DEMON D1051 UK PICTURE SLEEVE 7"

[1] *IWIWAL: I Wish I Was a Lesbian;*
[2] *TSDHAV: This Song Don't Have a Video*

Associated Releases

Airways (Paul Brady) and The Home of Donegal (trad)
Back to Centre,
Paul Brady (LWiii backing vocals)
UK MERCURY MERH 86

At the End of a Long Lonely Day (Smith Family)
From Hell to Obscurity,
Various Artists (LWiii duet with John Hiatt)
AK BLACKMAIL BLACK CD 1

Baltimore Fire (trad)
The McGarrigle Hour
(Various Artists LWiii featured)
RYKODISC/HANNIBAL HNCD 1417

Bill of Goods
Best of the Mountain Stage vol 1,
(Various Artists)
1991 US BLUE PLATE MUSIC BPM 001 CD

Colours
From Hell to Obscurity,
(Various Artists)
AK BLACKMAIL BLACK CD 1

Dead Skunk
Have a Nice Day:Super Hits of the Seventies Vol 10;
1990 RHINO

Dead Skunk
Hitchin' a Ride:Seventies Greatest Rock Vol 10;
1990 PRIORITY

Dead Skunk
Dr. Demento Presents ... Vol 4:The Seventies;
RHINO

Don't Go
From Where You Are
Sloan Wainwright (LWiii duet)
WATERBUG WBG 0042

Glad 'n' Greasy
The Beat Farmers
The Beat Farmers (LWiii backing vocals)
UK DEMON VEX 5 (REISSUED 1990,DEMON FIEND CD 39)

Glad to See You've Got Religion
Sundown: Mellow Rock Hits of the Seventies
1997 RHINO

Glad to See You've Got Religion
Soft Rock Classics
(3 CD Boxed Set)
1998 RHINO

Golfin' Blues
Golf's Greatest Hits
Various Artists
1996 TEED OFF RECORDS BMG 0100582136-2

Gospel Ship, The (trad)
The Earl Scruggs Revue, anniversary special vol 1,
Various Artists (LWiii with Johnny Cash and Joan Baez)
1975

Green Green Rocky Road (trad)
The McGarrigle Hour
Various Artists (LWiii featured)
RYKODISC/HANNIBAL HNCD 1417

Heart Needs a Home, A (Richard Thompson)
Beat the Retreat, Songs of Richard Thompson
Various Artists (LWiii with Shawn Colvin)
CAPITOL 7243831 48226

Hey Hey My My (Neil Young)
The Slugger's Wife
Various Artists (mus. dir Quincy Jones)
(LWiii with Rebecca De Mornay)
SOUNDTRACK US MCA 5578

Associated Releases

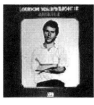

Album II
1971

I Eat Out
Life in the Folk Lane
Various Artists
1997 CD F722

Johnny's Gone to Hilo (trad)
The McGarrigle Hour
Various Artists (LWiii featured)
RYKODISC/HANNIBAL HNCD 1417

Little Drummer Boy (Davis/Onorati/Simeone)
John Schofield, Xmas Promo Single
(LWiii vocals)
VERVE RECORDS SACDVER 98

Little Red Corvette
The Slugger's Wife
Various Artists (mus. dir Quincy Jones),
(LWiii featured)
SOUNDTRACK US MCA 5578

Love The One You're With
The Slugger's Wife
Various Artists (mus. dir Quincy Jones),
(LWiii featured)
SOUNDTRACK US MCA 5578

My Girl
From Hell to Obscurity,
Various Artists (LWiii duet with John Hiatt)
AK BLACKMAIL BLACK CD 1

Old Friend
**Troubadours of Folk vol 4, Singer Song-
writers of the 70s**
Various Artists
US IMPORT RHINO R2 71843

Outsidey
Feed the Folk (Live at Edinburgh Festival)
Various Artists
UK TEMPLE FTP0792

Pack Up Your Sorrows
Bleecker Street:Greenwich Village in the Sixties
(LWiii Duet with Iris Dement)
1999

Schooldays
The McGarrigle Hour
Various Artists (LWiii featured)
RYKODISC/HANNIBAL HNCD 1417

Schooldays
The First Family of New Rock.
Various Artists

Swimming Song, The
**The Earl Scruggs Revue, anniversary
special vol 1,**
Various Artists
1975

Swimming Song/Pretty Little Martha/Dump the Dog
The Best of the Cambridge Folk Festival,
Various Artists,
STRANGE FRUIT/BBC CAFE CD 001

Swinging Bridge
Be Headed,
Chris Harford (LWiii backing vocals)
(1992) ELECTRA 9-61364-2

That's Enough for Me (Willie Nile)
Places I Have Never Been,
Willie Nile (LWiii backing vocals)
COLUMBIA CK 44434 CD

Virgin 21
Signed, Sealed and Delivered,
Virgin Records 21st anniversary CD
UK VIRGIN VVSAM 24

Waitress Song, The
Nyon Folk Festival
Various Artists
FRENCH PALEO GAD 0792 MUSIDISC-
EUROPE CAT 81004/81005

What'll I Do (Irving Berlin)
The McGarrigle Hour
Various Artists (LWiii featured)
RYKODISC/HANNIBAL HNCD 1417

Cover Versions

Motel Blues
Big Star
Big Star Live
RYKODISC RCD 10221, 1974

Hospital Lady
Glad to See You Got Religion
Uptown
School Days
Bruno's Place
Bruno's Place
The Bridge is Blue, 1972

The Man Who Couldn't Cry
Johnny Cash
American Recordings
AMERICAN 74321.23685.4, 1994

Be Careful There's a Baby in the House
The Establishment
1971

Swimming Song
Men
Fairport Convention
Old New Borrowed Blue
WOODWORM WRCD 024, 1996

Out of This World
Freakwater
Old Paint
CITY SLANG RECORDINGS CD CHICAGO EFA
04965-2

Swimming Song
Nic Jones
In Search of Nic Jones
MOLLIE MUSIC MMCD 01, 1998

Shurken (Mr Guilty)
Olga Magnell

Swimming Song
Kate and Anna McGarrigle
Kate and Anna McGarrigle
WARNER BROS 56218, 1975

School Days
Kate and Anna McGarrigle
The McGarrigle Hour
RYKODISC/ HANNIBAL HNCD 1417, 1998

Swimming Song
New Riders of the Purple Sage
New Riders of the Purple Sage
MCF 2758, 1976

Down Drinking at the Bar
Maura O'Connor

Swimming Song
Maddy Prior
A Year, 1993

Swimming Song
Eddi Reader

Dreaming
Norma Waterson
The Very Thought of You
HANNIBAL HNCD 1430, 1999

Ronnie Scott's, London 13 June1999

Photo: Lynn Westhead

*In 1998 Robbie Williams recorded Jesus in a Campervan, which quotes
from I am the Way, wrongly attributing it to I.Wiii, which resulted in a
lawsuit by the estate of Woody Guthrie

Unreleased

Air Travel — 1976
American Football — 1987
Back In The Bathroom — 1973
Ballad of Billy Gondola — 1979
Bed — 1998
Brave New Braver World — 1998
Bronx Girl Eileen — 1972
Button Nose — 1993
Detroit Is A Dying City — 1975
Dick And Jane — 1976
Edgar — 1968
Eight Bar Blues, The — 1976
Evening News — 1985
Everybody Knows I Want to Look Pretty — 1972
Father's Day Song — 1996
First Amendment Shuffle — 1990
Five Gold Stars — 1976
Flood of Tears — 1994
Girls, Girls *(with Geoffrey Bush)* — 1985
Hard Way, The *(with Geoffrey Bush)* — 1985
He Beat the Rap — 1994
Homeless — 1997
Hostess — 1971
Hotel Walls — 1985
I Am Saving my Blackheads for You — 1986
I Feel Strange *(with Geoffrey Bush)* — 1985
I Lost Again — 1998
I Love to Hear That K. C. When She Moans
(attr, Tee Wee Blackman)
I Shall Be Released *(Bob Dylan)* — 1974
I Walk Through the Graveyard — 1997
I Wonder if They Miss Us
I'm Not Gonna Cry — 1997
Intense Care — 1996
Intense Love — 1990
Is This What You've Done *(with Geoffrey Bush)* — 1985
Isn't Life Grand
Korean Song — 1975
Livin' On An Island — 1985
Living Alone — 1998
Love's Gifts — 1994

Mine's Not So Big — 1986
Missing the Nurses — 1974
Monkey in My Closet — 1976
Morning/Evening — 1989
MTV — 1984
My Biggest Fan — 1994
Newt Gingrich Is Running The Town — 1994
One Time in a Time — 1999
Out of Reach — 1998
POW (Prince of Wales) — 1997
Reagan Song — 1987
Really Me — 1994
Restlessness — 1981
Shit Song, The — 1995
Sink The Bismark — 1971
Skies, Eyes, Faces — 1994
So Good So Far — 1991
So Long John Sununu — 1994
Soldier's Last Letter, The *(Ernest Tubb?)*
Song about a Groupie
Sunday — 1985
Superbowl Sunday — 1987
Surfer Queen — 1984
Talking President Reagan — 1987
Thank You Mr. Hubble — 1996
Twist and Shout *(Isley Bros)* — 1976
Two Cups of Decaff — 1994
We'll Keep in Touch — 1998
Weave Room Blues
What You Go Through — 1989
White Winos — 1998
Will You Love Me — 1994
Wires in the Rug — 1989
Woodstock '94 — 1994
Working On My Ulcer — 1991
Wrong With My Act *(with Geoffrey Bush)* — 1985
You Kids Today — 1984
You Never Phone — 1994

Family and Friends

Kate and Anna McGarrigle
Kate and Anna McGarrigle
WARNER BROS K 56218, 1975

Dancer with Bruised Knees
Kate and Anna McGarrigle
WARNER BROS WB 56356, 1977

Pronto Monto
Kate and Anna McGarrigle
WARNER BROS K56561, 1978

The French Record
Kate and Anna McGarrigle
HANNIBAL HNBL 1302, 1980

Love Over and Over
Kate and Anna McGarrigle
POLYDOR POLS 1062, 1982

Heartbeats Accelerating
Kate and Anna McGarrigle
PRIVATE INC 261142, 1990

Matapedia
Kate and Anna McGarrigle
HANNIBAL HNCD 1394, 1997

The McGarrigle Hour
Kate and Anna McGarrigle
HANNIBAL HNCD 1417, 1998

The Roches
The Roches
WARNER BROS WB 56683, 1979

Nurds
The Roches
WARNER BROS K 56855, 1980

With Martha at the Lansdowne Playhouse, Boston, March 1996

Family and Friends

Keep on Doing
The Roches
WARNER BROS WB 57028, 1982

Another World
The Roches
WARNER BROS 1-25321, 1985

Speak
The Roches
MCA RECORDS MCG 6071, 1989

We Three Kings
The Roches
MCA RECORDS MCG 6122, 1990

Holy Smokes
Suzzy Roche
RED HOUSE, 1998

Obituary
George Gerdes
UNITED ARTISTS UAS 5549, 1971

Son of Obituary
George Gerdes
UNITED ARTISTS 5593, 1972

Sloan Wainwright
Sloan Wainwright
WATERBUG WBG, 1996

From Where You Are
Sloan Wainwright
WATERBUG WBG 0042, 1998

Rufus Wainwright
Rufus Wainwright
DREAMWORKS DRD 50039, 1998

Home Floor
Martha Wainwright
LIMITED EDITION (100) C90 TAPE, 1997

Photo from The McGarrigle Hour album cover

Kate and Anna McGarrigle, with family and friends

The song Little Ship is hopeful, it has a romantic strain to it.
But I've been really interested—
or obsessed really—with the family, and it's break-up, and what happened to it.
That's my subject, I guess:
What happened to the family?

DD/PI/13/3/98

Cuttings File

Melody Maker
1/4/71
Loudon: Sucking Songs from
the Cities
Andrew Means

Rolling Stone
29/4/71
A Tale of LWIII
Lenny Kaye

Melody Maker
16/10/71
The Man who made the
Speakeasy Listen
Roy Hollingworth

Melody Maker
1/11/74
Loudon Alone
Karl Dallas

Let It Rock
1/12/75
Busy Being Born
Graham Taylor

ZigZag Volume 6,#7
1/12/75
LWIII, A Short Biography
Jerry Gilbert

Melody Maker
22/9/79
Loudon is a Tuft Man
Colin Irwin

Magill
1/10/79
LW: A Live One
Gene Kerrigan

**International Musician &
Recording World**
1/11/79
LW and Being a Singer
Songwriter in 1979
Paul Ashford

Folk Roots #3
1/1/85

The Third Man
Colin Irwin

Musin' Music Magazine #3
11/9/85
LWIII Interview in Dublin
Rob O'Dempsey

Melody Maker
2/11/85
Shrink Rap
Loudon Wainwright

Pulse
1/6/89

Folk Roots #112
1/10/92
It's Historical
Colin Irwin

Mojo #2
1/12/93
Let's Hear it for. . .Me!
Jim White

Rock and Reel # 23
1/1/95
The Third Man
Rob O'Dempsey

Mojo
1/12/95
Identity Crisis
Loudon Wainwright

New York Times
7/1/96
Loudon Wainwright Still
Clearing the Air
Stephen Holden

Rolling Stone
26/10/72
Album iii Review
Stephen Holden

Q Magazine No 14
1/11/87
Exhaustive
Colin Shearman

Omaha Rainbow
1/4/88

The Independent on Sunday
27/9/92
Life is More than Dead Skunks
Ben Thompson

Musician
1/2/93
History Lessons

Goldmine
25/6/93
The Career Moves of LWiii
William Rushton

Breakfast All Day
August 1995
Illustrated Strip "Drinking Song"
Kevin Harrison

Glasgow Herald
25/9/95
Loudon Disorderly
David Belcher

Stereophile
1/7/96
A Grown Man
Steve Guttenberg

The Tracking Angle
1/6/96
From Dead Skunks to Lesbians
Steve Guttenberg

Songwriters on Songwriting
1/1/96
Interview with LWiii
Paul Zollo

Mojo
1/11/97
Suck on This
David Hepworth

**Hoot—25 Years of the
Greenwich Village music scene**
1/1/98
Robbie Woliver

JUNE 1986 No. 36 · £1.20

FOLK ROOTS

LOUDON WAINWRIGHT III

BRASS MONKEY

LEON ROSSELSON
DWIGHT YOAKAM
JIMMY CROWLEY
GONE TO EARTH

FEATURES ★ NEWS ★ REVIEWS

Wainwright is no poet, he's a songwriter. Which means putting words of intelligence, wit and occasionally passion to suitable music and making the combination work.

GK/MG/79

TV and Films

1972	**Old Grey Whistle Test**	BBC2, Live in studio, Liza/Down Drinkin' in the Bar	London
1974	**Mash guest appearance 2**	Cameo role in TV comedy - BBC2	USA
1974	**Saturday Night Live**	Live in Studio, Unrequited	N.Y.
1974	**Mash guest appearance 3**	Cameo role in TV comedy - BBC2	USA
1974	**Mash guest appearance 1**	Cameo role in TV comedy - BBC2	USA
1974	**Fernwood Tonight**	Live in Studio, Golfin' Blues	USA
16/7/75	**Marc Time**	Live in Studio, Detroit is a Dying City;	
		Unrequited to the Nth Degree	Aberdeen
3/12/76	**Rockpalast**	Live in Studio (65 mins)	Cologne
1/12/77	**Mike Douglas Show**	Live Set	USA
15/2/78	**Sight and Sound In Concert,**	Live Concert, Paris Theatre, Unrequited	London
6/7/78	**Merv Griffin Show**	Live in Studio, B side/Golfin' Blues	USA
1/7/79	**Cambridge Folk Festival**	Four numbers from LWiii's set, BBC TV	Cambridge
1980	**Causeway Folk**	Live set, BBC TV NI	Portrush
12/11/80	**Good Evening Ulster**	Live in Studio, Say That You Love Me	Belfast
1/1/81	**Leidercircus**	Live in Studio with the Roches, Vampire Blues	Germany
22/11/81	**Robert Klein Show**	Live in Studio, Rumbunctious/Grammy Song	USA
1982	**Old Grey Whistle Test**	Live in Studio, Ingenue/Dump the Dog, BBC2	London
1/4/83	**Old Grey Whistle Test**	Live in Studio, IDTTYWLM, BBC2	London
11/11/84	**Rockpalast-Zeche**	Live Concert, WDR repeated December 1995 (75 mins)	Bochum
1985	**The Corries**	Live in Studio	Scotland
1985	**WEDU Tampa**	Concert and Interview, (58 mins)	Tampa
1985	**The Slugger's Wife**	Feature film dir. Hal Ashbury, cameo role and soundtrack	
26/7/85	**About Anglia**	Live in Studio, Cardboard boxes + chat, ITV regional	Norwich
20/8/85	**Wogan**	Live in Studio, Cardboard Boxes, BBC1 TV chat show	London
12/10/85	**Corries TV Show**	Live in Studio	Dublin
29/10/85	**Whistle Test**	Live in Studio, Hard Day On The Planet, BBC2	London
24/4/86	**Cambridge Folk Festival**	Live set, Hard Day/Five Years Old, Anglia TV	Cambridge
13/5/86	**Ohne Filter**	As part of John Hiatt's set, German TV	Baden Baden
13/5/86	**Ohne Filter**	Solo set in Studio, German TV	Baden Baden
2/9/86	**The Arts Programme**	Live in Studio, Unhappy Anniversary, BBC2	London
1987	**Austin City Limits**	Live set, US TV	Austin
3/1/87	**Carrott Confidential**	Live in Studio, Surfin' Queen, BBC1 TV	London
10/1/87	**Carrott Confidential**	Live in Studio, Talkin' President, BBC1 TV	London
17/1/87	**Carrott Confidential**	Live in Studio, You Don't Want to Know, BBC1 TV	London
24/1/87	**Carrott Confidential**	Live in Studio, Superbowl Sunday, BBC1 TV	London
31/1/87	**Carrott Confidential**	Live in Studio, Nocturnal Stumblebutt, BBC1 TV	London
7/2/87	**Carrott Confidential**	Live in Studio, Unrequited to the Nth Degree, BBC1	London
14/2/87	**Carrott Confidential**	Live in Studio, IDTTYWLM, BBC1 TV	London
21/2/87	**Carrott Confidential**	Live in Studio, Saw You on TV, BBC1 TV	London
2/11/87	**Six Tonight**	Interview with Ronan Kelly, Ulster TV	Belfast

The problem with acting is that I don't really have a position in the acting world. I really have to get out there and compete with every taxi-driver and waiter in New York (WR/Gold/25/6/93)

TV and Films

It's taken nearly 20 years to go from Spalding MD to balding MC but the wait has been well worth it

(BD/TO)

7/11/87	The Late Late Show	Live in Studio, Unhappy Anniversary, RTE	Dublin
1989	Jacknife	Feature film starring Robert de Niro, dir. David Jones cameo role as Vietnam vet	
1989	Pinnacle The Movie, Having Your Cake	They Spelt My Name Wrong, Pinnacle Records Promo	London
15/10/89	Night Music	Live TV , Jesse Don't Like It +1 (With Pere Ubu)	New York
1990	New Vision	Live in studio, Aphrodisiac, US TV	USA
1/7/90	MTV News	Feature, Jesse Don't Like It, US TV	USA
1/7/90	The Tonight Show	Live, I Wanna Be on MTV, US TV	Los Angeles
13/7/90	The Tonight Show	Live in Studio, I Wanna Be on MTV	Los Angeles
1992	Soldier, Soldier	Cameo role in TV drama series (Central Video)	UK
15/10/92	Later with Jools Holland	Live in Studio, The Doctor/Hitting You + chat, BBC2	London
16/10/92	Anderson On The Box	Live in Studio, The Picture/Men + chat, BBC NI	Belfast
1993	As The World Turns	Cameo role in US feature film, Dutch TV	USA
1993	Family Affairs	Live in Studio, The Picture, BBC1	London
26/1/93	Conan O'Brien Show	Live in Studio, He Said She Said/IWIWAL	NY
28/2/93	Dutch TV on children	Live in Studio, Dutch VPRO	Holland
28/5/93	One Man Guy	Dutch TV Documentary, features interviews with LWiii, Kate McGarrigle, Rufus and Martha, plus song excerpts. (60 minutes)	Holland
9/12/93	The Late Show	Live in Studio, Career Moves/Suddenly It's Xmas, BBC2	London
9/4/94	Words & Music	Talks about and sings Thanksgiving, BBC2 documentary	London
9/6/94	Cambridge Folk Festival	Whatever Happened To US/Cardboard Boxes, Anglia TV	Cambridge
13/7/94	Loudon and Co	Host to show + live He Said She Said, BBC2	Glasgow
20/7/94	Loudon and Co	Host to show + live I'm Alright, BBC2	Glasgow
29/7/94	Loudon and Co	Host to show + live Talkin' New Bob Dylan/Mr Guilty, BBC2	Glasgow
3/8/94	Loudon and Co	Host to show + live Unhappy Anniversary, BBC2	Glasgow
10/8/94	Loudon and Co	Host to show + live Swimming Song, BBC2	Glasgow
3/10/94	The Midday Show	I'd Rather Be Lonely + chat, Australian channel 9	Melbourne
4/11/95	Kenny Live	Live in Studio, Grown Man, Irish RTE	Dublin
16/12/95	Take It To The Bridge	Interview + live in studio, What Gives, VH-1	London
18/1/96	Conan O'Brien Show	Live in Studio, Grown Man	NY
28/10/97	Jack Docherty Show	Live in Studio, Breakfast in Bed + chat. Channel 5	London
1/11/97	Kenny Live	Live in Studio, OGM	Dublin
1998	Mission Impossible	Feature film starring Tom Cruise, cameo role as 'suit'.	
1999	28 Days	Feature film starring Sandra Bullock, cameo role as rehab client in drug and alcohol clinic, plus soundtrack	

[In Owners at the Young Vic] I played a character who keeps trying to kill himself but can't pull it off...typecasting!

(RO'D/MMM/1987)

BBC Radio

23/05/71
John Peel
Sink the Bismark!, School Days, Be Careful
There's a Baby In The House, East Indian
Princess, Four Is a Magic Number

3/10/71
John Peel
Say That You Love Me, Samson and The
Warden, Motel Blues, Trilogy (Circa 1967),
Plane, Too

08/11/71
Bob Harris
Drinking Song, Glenvillle Reel, Bronx Girl
Eileen, Hey Packy, Motel Blues, Dead Skunk,
Four Is a Magic Number

2/06/73
John Peel
Clockwork Chartreuse, a.M. World, Down
Drinking at The Bar, I am the Way, Lullaby

12/05/75
John Peel
Bicentennial, Detroit's a Dying City, Unre-
quited To The Nth Degree, Hollywood
Hopeful, Have You Ever Been To Pittsburgh?,
Five Gold Stars.

1975
In Concert
Bicentennial, I am The Way, Have You Ever
Been To Pittsburgh?, Unrequited to the Nth
Degree, absence Makes The Heart Grow
Fonder, B/Side, Hollywood Hopeful,
RedGuitar, Just Like President Thieu, Surfing
Queen, Motel Blues, Muse Blues, Dilated to
Meet You, Old Paint, School Days, Whatever
Happened To Us?, Bellbottom Pants, Suicide
Song, Clockwork Chartreuse.

26/08/76
John Peel
Ingenue, Golfin' Blues, The Swimming Song,
Prince Hal's Dirge

09/12/76.
John Peel
Natural Disaster, air Travel, Monkey In My
Closet, Dick and Jane, It's Over The Hill, My
Girl

13/08/79.
John Peel
Saturday Morning Fever, The acid Song,
Vampire Blues, april Fool's Day Morn, Dump
The Dog

14/04/83.
John Peel
Outsidey, I'm alright, Screaming Issue, Career
Moves, Not John

23/04/83
In Concert
Final Exam, I'm alright, Five Years Old,
Revenge, I.D.T.T.Y.W.L.M, Golfin' Blues, B/
Side, Mr. Guilty, Unrequited To The Nth
Degree, Vampire Blues, Fear of Flying,
Plane,Too, Samson and The Warden, Fame and
Wealth, Saturday Morning Fever, Kings and
Queens, Prince Hal's Dirge, Dead Skunk

30/09/85
John Peel
Expatriot, No, You Kids Today, I Wanna Be on
MTV, Hard Day on The Planet, Synchronicity

01/10/87
Andy Kershaw
Me and all the Other Mothers, aphrodisiac,
You Don't Want to Know, Harry's Wall

Sessions

19/10/89
John Peel
T.S.M.N.W.A, Jessie Don't Like It, Sunday Times, Sometimes I Forget

08/01/90
Kaleidoscope
Interview; You Don't Want To Know, a Handful Of Dust, Synchronicity, I Eat Out, Your Mother and I, Motel Blues, The Home Stretch

04/02/93
Kaleidoscope
Inaugural Blues, Talkin' New Bob Dylan, Hitting You

31/07/93
Johnny Walker
That Hospital, I Wish I Was a Lesbian, I Suppose

14/08/93
Andy Kershaw
It's Love and I Hate It, I Suppose, I Eat Out, I.D.T.T.W.LM, I Wish I Was a Lesbian, School Days, That Hospital, One Man Guy

15/08/93
John Peel
A Father and a Son, Colours, Be Careful There's a Baby in The House, Just a John, Between

15/10/95
Andy Kershaw
Cobwebs, I Suppose, What are Families For?, Treasures Untold, The Shit Song, Our Own War, Lullaby, Fame and Wealth

20/10/95
Kaleidoscope
Swimming Song, The Human Cannonball

13/10/97
Andy Kershaw
I'm Not Gonna Cry, O.G.M, Bein' a Dad, What Gives?, Homeless, So Damn Happy, Little Ship, a Song

13/10/97
Richard allinson
(BBC Radio 2) Primrose Hill, Our Own War

29/7/99
LWiii Live in John Peel's Living Room
4 songs plus chat:
When I'm at Your House; Be Careful There's a Baby in the House; One Time at a Time (new song from film "28 days", at the End of a Long Lonely Day (Smith Family/Marty Robbins)

Some of Those...

2001
Title of SF Novel by Arthur C. Clarke, and film by Stanley Kubrick
Y2K
Audie Murphy
War hero and Singing Cowboy
Bicentennial
Audrey/Katherine
actresses Audrey Hepburn (known for classic ingenue roles) and Katherine Hepburn (known for stroppy, feisty roles)
Ingenue
Captain Nemo
Captain of the submarine *Nautilus* in *20000 Leagues Under the Sea* by Jules Verne
Man's World
Charlie can't help her
Charles Manson, leader of fanatical hippy cult in California, convicted of conspiracy to commit the savage murder of actress Sharon Tate, wife of Roman Polanski
California Prison Blues
Clockwork Chartreuse
ref to *A Clockwork Orange* by Anthony Burgess, made into film by Stanley Kubrick
Clockwork Chartreuse
Cummerbund
Broad sash or waistband worn with Dinner jacket/Tuxedo
Westchester County
Dave Clark Five
60s British beat group from Tottenham, North London
What Gives
Eldridge
Eldridge Cleaver, spokesman for Black Panther party
California Prison Blues
Emmanuel Zacchini Sr.
Circus Human Cannonball,(1909-1993), made

record-breaking 175ft,54ft flight in 1940
Human Cannonball
Foster Brooks
Actor, associated with alcoholism, famous for portrayal of loveable lush
Wine with Dinner
Gerry
Gerry and the Pacemakers, 60s British Merseyside beat group
What Gives
Hal the computer
See 2001
Y2k
Handful of Dust
*A Handful of Dust :*Title of 1934 novel by Evelyn Waugh
Handful of Dust
Hank Junior/Senior
Hank Williams Junior sang on one of the first records and videos manipulated to include a dead person, in this case his father
What Gives
Hardy Boys
Eponymous boy-detective heros of series of adventure books for teenagers by W. Handy
Hardy Boys at the Y
He Said, She Said
title of film starring Kevin Bacon
He Said, She Said
Help me Rhonda
Help Me Rhonda, 1965 Beach Boys song
Wine with Dinner
Herman
Herman's Hermits, 60s British beat group
What Gives
Ides of March
Date of assassination of Julius Caesar; "Beware the Ides of March!" *Julius Caesar*, (1.ii.18) Shakespeare
Me and My Friend the Cat

...References

Jack Ruby
Dallas nightclub owner and petty criminal, who murdered Lee Harvey Oswald who was in custody accused of Kennedy assassination.
Bicentennial
Jesse
Jesse Helm, Republican Senator for North Carolina, opponent of National Endowment for the Arts
John Donne wasn't lying
John Donne 1572-1631; Metaphysical Poet "No man is an island, entire of itself", *Devotions*
Hard Day on the Planet
John Sununu
Republican Congressman for new Hampshire, and former White House Chief of Staff
So Long John Sununu
Liza
actress Liza Minelli, daughter of Judy Garland and Vicente Minelli
Liza
Manfred Mann
Manfred Mann,60s British beat group
What Gives
Maynard G. Krebs
Fictional spoof beatnik played by Bob Denver in 1959 US TV comedy show *The Many Loves of Dobie Gillis*
Cobwebs
Mr. Steinbeck
John Steinback, author of the *Grapes of Wrath* (see Tom Joad)
Trilogy (Circa 1967)
Olga Korbutt
Soviet gymnast, gold medallist in 1972 Olympics
Tonya's Twirls
Paint
Spotted horse or pony; Pinto

Old Paint
Patricia/Patty
Patty Hearst, daughter of Newspaper magnate William Randolph Hearst, kidnapped by 'Symbionese Liberation Army' 1974, and later took part in armed robbery with captors; jailed but released after 2 years
California Prison Blues
Phil Donahue
US T.V. chat show host
Man's World
Praise the Lord and pass the ammo
quotation from Howell Forgy, American naval chaplain, who said "Praise the Lord and pass the ammunition" as he moved along a chain of sailors passing ammunition hand to hand at Pearl Harbour. Later used as title of a song by Frank Loesser
Ready or Not (So Ripe)
President Thieu
Nguyen Van Unen Thieu, President of S. Vietnam, 1967-1975, in Europe for 1972 peace talks.
Just like President Thieu
Prince Hal
future King Henry V, as referred to in *King Henry IV* parts i and ii by Shakespeare, both of which contain innumerable references to taverns, capons, bottles of sack, rogues and wenches
Prince Hal's Dirge
Shuffle off this mortal coil
"When we have shuffled off this mortal coil" *Hamlet,* (3.i.66) Shakespeare
I Know I'm Unhappy
Simon Legree
Villainous slave-owner in *Uncle Tom's Cabin* (1852) by Harriet Beecher Stowe
Nice Guys
Squeaky's in prison
Lynette 'Squeaky' Fromm, member of Charles

Manson 'family' (see 'Charlie'), attempted to assassinate Gerald Ford
California Prison Blues
Stanley Cup
Ice Hockey's NHL "holy grail", established 1892
Just like President Thieu
Sweet parting sorrow
"Parting is such sweet sorrow" *Romeo and Juliet*, (2.ii.184) Shakespeare
Old Friend
Tania
pseudonym of Patty Hearst
California Prison Blues
Thomas Naguchi
Famous Los Angeles Coroner
Revenge
Timothy
Timothy Leary, sixties cult figure, advocate of

psychedelic drugs, and author of *The Politics of Ecstasy*
California Prison Blues
Tom Joad
Character in *The Grapes of Wrath* (1939) by John Steinbeck. Also Woody Guthrie song, *The Ballad of Tom Joad*
Road Ode
Tonya
Tonya Harding, Olympic figure skater
Tonya's Twirls
Vladimir and Estragon
Characters from *Waiting for Godot* (1952) by Samuel Beckett
Road Ode
Willie Loman
Principal character in *Death of a Salesman*, by Arthur Miller
Road Ode

Photo: Lynn Westhead

Index of First Lines

Index of First Lines

Index of First Lines

Index of First Lines

He Said, They Said

An anthology of quotations

Accolades

LWiii's wit is as dry as the Mojave and as sharp as the crease in a bond-trader's pants. His face is made of pure neoprene, and he's got the best comic timing in the singer-songwriter business.
Steve Guttenberg, *Stereophile*, July 1996

His songs are generally perceptive, autobiographical works that are peppered with a quirky, sly humour which allows a startling honesty not often heard in such palatable form.
Modern Dance Review, #18

One of the greatest songwriters alive… Nothing can compare to the joy you'll experience by attending his all-round-entertainment live show.
Paint in Red (UK)

While his forte is lyrics Wainwright composes excellent melodies and this exhibits an uncanny knack for matching form with content.
Jay Fialkov, *The One and Only Loudon Wainwright*, November 1996

Loudon's natural environment is the stage, alone with his guitar, the audience in the palm of his hand.
Steve Guttenberg, *The Tracking Angle*, Summer 1996

If you have loved, hated, been drunk, fought with your relatives, fantasised about sex or worried about modern life, then you are in at least several of his songs. If you cannot relate to many of Wainwright's songs then there is one piece of advice: Get a Life.
Brian Wise, *Mojo*, December 1994

Loudon Wainwright is one of the most side-splitting, heartbreaking songwriters working today.
Independent on Sunday

A great singing storyteller, he still projects the slightly scary radarlike vision of a precocious brat who sees through all disguises, including his own, and feels compelled to tattle on everybody.
Steven Holden, T*he Sunday New York Times*

Loudon Wainwright III's last album 'Therapy'. The guy is just incredible. I wish I'd kept his first two albums. But this last album was a work of complete genius.
Adrian Deevoy, "Bob Geldof's Record Collection", *Q* magazine

Loudon Wainwright is blessed with a rare gift; one that enables him to write three or four minute masterpieces which, while often making you laugh out loud, also have an incredible thought-provoking honesty
Dave Haslam, *Rock and Reel*, Spring 1998

Birth and Death

"I used to write songs about lousy relationships…now it's about death and disease; you gotta move on
Toronto Globe and Mail, 15 March 1996

"When did I grow up? When my father died in 1988…That's when you get the grown-ups' wake-up call. Freud said that the death of a parent was the single most important event in adult life, and it was certainly mind-blowing for me. I was left wrestling with the idea of feeling like a child…who's looking forward to death and decay."
David Belcher, *Glasgow Herald*, 29 September 1995

"Oh I just write about it. It keeps me balanced. I'm not going to commit suicide. You're not going to get rid of me that easily. You figure you're going to die anyway, so why rush it? But I'm looking forward to it. it's an exciting prospect."
Colin Irwin, *Folk Roots*, June 1986

Britain

"I'm a club act. I'm a national club act, but a club act…Now in Britain I can do concerts, which is one of the reasons that I've spent a lot of time there. I can do a hall in London or a hall in Edinburgh or a hall in Birmingham or Belfast or Dublin. So that's kind of an ego thing, and fun and good for the pocketbook too.

William Ruhlman, *Goldmine*, June 1993

"If there's one person I owe my career to in this country it's John Peel"

Colin Irwin, *Folk Roots*, June 1986

David Mansfield

of all the musicians Loudon has worked with, Mansfield is his most sympatico accompanist; his touch is never less than magical

Steve Guttenberg, *The Tracking Angle*, Summer 1996

Dead Skunk

This brought a brief glimpse of the big time—getting picked up in limousines to go and judge skunk contests... "In a way that's kind of a cool thing to be remembered for— I'd rather have a hit single about a dead skunk than 'I miss you, let's go to the mountains', or 'Colorado you're the best'. Dead animals are forever. When I made my next album they said 'This is good, but where's the funny animal song?'"

Ben Thompson, *Independent on Sunday*, September 1992

Dead Skunk was a huge hit in 1972. In Little Rock Arkansas it was No. 1 for six weeks in a row. "Bill Clinton must have a copy" Wainwright thinks, "I'm sure his whole presidency is predicated on it. I should've been offered a Cabinet position"

Jim White, *Mojo*

Dylan

"I was playing at Max's, Kansas City and I'd just written the Dead Skunk song, and he came backstage with Doug Sahm and said something like 'it's a good song the skunk song'...so Bob knows a hit when he hears one!"

Colin Irwin, Folk Roots #19

"Everyone who picked up a guitar in those days was a new Bob Dylan."

Gene Kerrigan, *Magill*, October 1979

Loudon can pinpoint the exact moment when he decided to make music his career. He was watching Bob Dylan at America's Newport Folk Festival in 1962. "I was eating a peanut butter sandwich and the earth moved."

Programme notes for Cambridge Corn Exchange concert.

Early Career Moves

"Well my version of 'Why Must I Be a Teenager in Love' was 'Why Must I Be a 21 Year Old Who Can't Get Laid and Who Beats Off a Lot' explains Wainwright. "That's why I wanted to get into show business. Isn't that why everyone wants to?"

Jim White, *Mojo*

"My first two albums were critically, I would say, overpraised, in retrospect, and then on my third album I had a kind of novelty hit single on it. Then, when my fourth album came along and there was no hit single it was like, 'well that's over, we can get on to the next one. Oh look, here comes Steve Forbert.'"

Fame

The fame I had with *Dead Skunk* was revolting in some ways, horrible, I hated it. It was grotesque, then my career haemorrhaged.

Steve Guttenberg, *Stereophile*, July 1996

"It was almost like an attempt to obliterate that success. In many ways that success freaked me out. Success is scary. Almost scarier than failing. Failing is frightening, but succeeding is *really* frightening. I suppose I do have a certain aversion to success, but it's a case of pacing yourself. I wanna be in showbiz when I'm 60 years old, barring accidents or premature death or a plane-crash. I hope to be in showbiz in one form or another until the day I die, so in a way it's a

mixed blessing not to be a huge success. I've been successful in many ways on my own terms. By failing.
Colin Irwin, *Melody Maker*, September 1979

"During *Dead Skunk* I was going everywhere in limos; there were 14 year old people pressing their faces against the windows." he says. "It scared the shit out of me, the fact my life going to be taken away from me. And I have a theory, that I didn't have—this is a therapy term—I didn't have permission to embrace success. Permission is granted or withheld from one's father. He had a problem with success and failure. He was very successful, on one level, running a great magazine, admired by his peers, but he didn't write books and he was very hung up by that. It was the drama and in the end the tragedy of his life. He could'nt accept the fact that he wasn't John Updike or Norman Mailer or Saul Bellow. He drove himself nuts about it, ragged himself. When I got it, or something like it, he didn't like it. Why should he? But in the end I just bailed out."
Jim White, *Mojo*

"The truth of the matter is, people who are singers or actors or writers, or painters, or architects or doctors—they want to make it, they want to become known, they want to make money. They want to be loved. This is the driving force of the human condition. Show business people *really* want to be loved. I've written about it my whole career. My desire for it, my revulsion about it or towards it, my need for it, my frustration about not getting it. I was 25 when it happened to me. It kind of blew me away. I don't yearn for a #1 record, but maybe I want those faces pressed up on that limo to be, you know, 30 year old women. I don't know…why should I be coy about this? *20*

year old women, or 45 year old intellectuals; I'll take a wide spectrum of people, including the 14 year old kids."
Steve Guttenberg, *Stereophile*, July 1996

"You wanna know who my favourite beatle was? Stu Sutcliffe."
Melody Maker, November 1985

Family

"It is one of the most extraordinary things in a man's life to find himself turning into his father."
Jim White, *Mojo*

"My father went to the same school. It fucked him up so he sent me there too."
LWiii in concert, Royal Festival Hall, 1993

'This is your father, this is you, and you're not as good.' Whereas the public doesn't have such an ingrained knowledge of my parents. I feel guilty because it's helped me more than anything; it's gotten me exposure
Rufus Wainwright, *Telegraph Magazine*, 1998

"There's a story in the family of my father being with his parents on a trip to europe with other family members in 1929, and the men coming in and and saying 'pack the trunks, we've got to go. Wall Street's just crashed. We lost eight million dollars today'"
Jim White, *Mojo*

Early home life , he remembers, was dominated by his father. "Well actually the house was dominated by his absence. He was always at work. It wasn't a happy marriage. There weren't any huge, Eugene O'Neil ructions, nobody was shooting morphine in secret, although there was a lot of drinking going on."
Jim White, *Mojo*

"The song *Little Ship* is hopeful, it has a romantic strain to it. But I've been really interested—or obsessed, really—with the family, and its break-up, and what happened

He Said, They Said

to it. That's my subject I guess: What happened to the family?"
Don Deluca, *Philadelphia Inquirer,* March 1998

First Guitar

"My father gave me my first guitar. Actually there was a bit of a competition; he had a guitar and didn't take to it, or didn't learn how to play it or something. And between my brother and sister and me he said 'whoever learns to play this I'll give it to them'. He encouraged that kind of sibling rivalry and I jumped at the chance and I got the ax. I was 13 years old."
Kaleidoscope, BBC 4, 1989

Guitar Style

"I write simple melodies and I incorporate the 10 guitar chords I learned when I was 15 and still use today."
Daryl Morden, *Pulse,* October 1989

Loudon's guitar playing is so good, yet I've never seen it referred to in reviews. Loud's tunes are simple, never demanding, but his rythm and phrasing fit so perfectly, maybe that's why no one notices.
Steve Guttenberg, *The Tracking Angle,* Summer 1996

"I began playing guitar imitating Ramblin' Jack Elliott but it's still pretty basic. I can play three songs on the Piano" he adds proudly, then breaks into a grin "all in the same key."

"Technically I'm not a good musician. I know a few chords, I can play on the

guitar and I have a good right hand, but I'm not working on my musical development. I'm not taking guitar lessons or anything."
Ted Joseph, *Sounds,* July 1976

Interviews

How Old Are You is Loudon'd anti-interview song. Having just arrived in Ireland a jet-lagged LWiii went through one gruelling such interview, live on radio with an interviewer he later described as 'not having a clue', who for twenty minutes asked such pertinent questions as 'are you a sex symbol?'…Finally Loudon was asked what

Photo: Lynn Westhead

68

musicians did he look up to. Loudon answered "well I like David Byrne, have you heard of him?" No. "He's a musician. Have you heard of Tom Petty?" No. "He's a musician. Have you heard of Engelbert Humperdinck?" Yes. "Well I don't look up to him at all!"

Rob O'Dempsey, *Musin' Music* magazine

Money

"The albums that I make are not expensive. What I spent on this one would probably pay for a Guns and Roses deli platter."

Ben Thompson, *Independent on Sunday*, September 1992

"The whole business of music is very youth-orientated, but for 25 years I've managed to eke out a pretty good living. It's paid the Child Support payments."

Colin Irwin, *Folk Roots* #19

" I have an advantage without a band in performance, and I don't have to divide that money up five ways."

Mike Flood Page, *Album Tracking*, 1977

Performances

"The first concert was with the Everly Brothers, who on that occasion had a purist grease and bicycle-chain crowd who didn't take kindly to a guy with an acoustic guitar singing about babies and suicide."

Rob Mackie, *Sounds*

He confesses that he is happiest on stage, and it shows. "It's just the outside world I have a few problems dealing with."

Brian Wise, Mojo December 1994

"I'm a natural performer. When I was seven I discovered that I liked showing off. When there's 2000 people in the dark watching you and the lights are all on you, I find that delightful"

Nigel Williamson, The Times, 24 November 1997

Other vocal demands from the audience brought flashes of the old Wainwright wit. A

hippy who shouted '*I am the Way*' was told by the singer "Congratulations".

Terry Kelly, Live at East Durham Community Theatre, 15 November 1996

Loudon Wainwright is the last troubador. When he arrives in Britain for a concert tour he comes without a comfort blanket of security advisors, sound-check executives and personal fitness supervisors. He steps off the plane from the States alone, hires a car at the airport, slings his guitar and black attaché case in the boot and sets off to Leeds, Belfast, Dublin or Edinburgh. Once there he plugs in his guitar, plays for 90 minutes and then disappears into a back room where he insists on receiving his fee in used notes, items he slips into his attaché case before heading off again in his hire car.

Jim White, *Mojo*

Richard Thompson

Richard is great fun, a hilarious man, he does wonderful impressions, accents, he keeps everybody laughing, and he's just a little bit better than me at tennis. Not much."

Steve Guttenberg, *Stereophile*, July 1996

Songs and Songwriting

Where do these songs come from? *The Birthday Present* was recorded while you were taking a shower—is that where you were when you wrote it?

"No, I was bone dry and fully clothed when I wrote that one. I write songs everywhere—in a car, a plane, or yes, in the shower. I get up in the middle of the night and scribble something down. I'm always out there fishing for something…and you *could* catch something in the shower."

Steve Guttenberg, *Stereophile*, July 1996

"I can push it to the limit. An example of that would be the hospital song [*That Hospital*] where I'm talking about an abortion. In a live

situation you can actually hear the audience gasp sometimes—it's just a little close."
Steve Guttenberg, *Stereophile*, July 1996

He has devoted songs to a variety of subjects not otherwise touched on in the whole history of songwriting: moving; eating in restaurants by yourself; the life of a bee; swimming; golf; bell-bottom pants; the difficulty of getting on with one's friend's wife; making an overseas call and of course, a dead skunk in the middle of the road...
"I think the politics of relationships, of men and women, of parenting, of guilt, of obsession. There's a politic in that and these are the politics that I address."
William Ruhlman, *Goldmine*, July 1993

"Well lesbians is a happening thing...I suppose I'm just cashing in on the whole thing".
You seem as a writer to be able to get away with writing songs about very touchy topics, like lesbianism. Very few people would get away with it, why do you think that is?
"Because I handle the subjects with such delicacy."
Rob O Dempsey, *Rock and Reel #23*, 1995

Wainwright is no poet, he's a songwriter. Which means putting words of intelligence, wit and occasionally passion to suitable music and making the combination work.
Gene Kerrigan, *MaGill*, 1979

"Well maybe they didn't misinterpret it. Maybe I am putting him down. I just don't know if I am or if I'm not. It was just one of those things that came out. I once did an interview with Bob Geldof actually when he was a journalist. He was a fucking snake, so there may be some truth in it."
William Ruhlman, *Goldmine*, June 1993

"I'm an exhibitionist or a masochist. The rule of writing is to write about what you know and I'm obsessed with myself. It's not necessarily a good thing, but that's what I do. I get off on showing the warts..."
"The artful thing is to take that self-absorption and fashion it into a three-minute song that can engage other people..."
"You don't think 'let's add some more irony here' when you're writing a song. The low humour I use is just part of my style. But Freud said the joke is a way of allowing the unconscious to talk safely about horrible things. That's why you explode with laughter: because you're touched with something deep..."
"Since I am writing about sensitive subjects the humour can leaven it and make it less dreary..."
Nigel Williamson, *The Times*, October 1997

Writing he says is like fishing: "You're sitting out there in the boat for hours, but when you've got one it doesn't take long to land it. I'm fishing all the time, but I can go long periods with nothing, then a batch of them come along".
Nigel Williamson, *The Times*, October 1997

"I like to be on the road, because I consider myself a better performer than anything else. I'm also an excellent songwriter. A brilliant songwriter for that matter. I'm also a genius in the studio." He outright laughed then recovered his seriousness. "But I ain't no Stevie Wonder, or Paul McCartney for that matter
Ted Joseph, *Sounds*, July 1976

"When it's going well things come easily. You don't labour too much about what rhymes with what. It's like a jigsaw puzzle where you just start finding pieces. It's when you're sitting there thinking about what rhymes with 'chair' that you know it's time to stop"

Jon Garelick, *Come in Loudon*, 1998

Loudon is remarkably precise in his use of words; the accuracy of his language is somehow made effective because he doesn't often try to be obviously intelligent. He has the knack of implying a strong melodic line without necessarily staying close to it. And Loudon's acoustic guitar playing is really exciting, full of surprising crescendos and stops in rhythm

Charlie Gillett, *Folk Roots*

Themes

Inevitably more love songs finds Wainwright tilling familiar ground. I suspect that his albums will now always be litanies of increasing bitterness about his estrangement from his former wives, his interminable failures with women, his persistent worries about his worth as an artist, a man, a father.

Allan Jones, *Melody Maker*, October 1986

The heros is Wainwright's songs are all permanently flawed—they are cheats, losers, drunks, cowards, insane and deadbeat. But the more extreme their weaknesses the greater his sympathy.

Allan Jones, *Melody Maker*, April 1978

Therapy

"I'm back where I grew up in Westchester County. Real Commuter country. All the guys take the train to the city every day. I go in a couple of times to see my shrink."

Does your shrink listen to your records?

"There wouldn't be any reason to go if he heard the records. I could save myself a lot of money if I did that. When he's cured me I can say 'look, this is what I was like before'. I like to write about myself and I'm prepared to pay for that pleasure and privilege."

David Hepworth, *Mojo*, 1998

"I have a competetive relationship with almost everyone. Actually," he says pointing to my lunch plate, "I think I had a better appetiser than you did."

Jim White, Mojo,

Vietnam

"I dropped out of school, lived at home and had to deal with the draft" he recalls of the days when student deferment was all that stood between many young men and Vietnam "and thought for a while about enlisting, and actually did enlist, or sign up for the Airborne, the guys that jump out of the planes. This is prime Vietnam War time. But the day I was supposed to go in and be sworn in I actually overslept. My unconscious mind took over and I missed the swearing-in ceremony. Then I thought about it, and decided to take my chances with the draft. By that time I was seeing a psychiatrist, and was classified as 'socio-psychopath' I think they called it. So the shrink got me out of the army, basically."

William Ruhlman, *Goldmine*, July 1993

"I avoided the Vietnam draft, another thing where rich kids get off the hook. Actually if you were white and at all educated you got off the draft"

Did Bob Dylan get out of the draft?

"You bet your ass."

Jim White, Mojo

Who?

A weird combination of Tommy Smothers, James Taylor and Ogden Nash

Toronto Gobe and Mail, 15 March 1996

One of the best humorous songwriters since the days of Tom Lehrer

Nigel Williamson, Times 24 October 1997

He is the Alan Clark of the songwriting world.

Nigel Williamson, Times 24 October 1997

"I wasn't the new Bob Dylan any more, I was now the Woody Allen of Folk, the Charlie Chaplin of Rock and, my favourite, the male Melanie."
Phil Sutcliffe, *Q* magazine, April 1991

The most misspelled name in popular music.
Edinburgh Festival handout

The Tom Lehrer of Rock and Roll, Wainwright has the potential to become its Jonathan Swift.
Kit Rachlis, *LP Review*

"The very first new Bob Dylan rapidly becoming the Old Steve Forbert."
Andy Kershaw, BBC 13 October 1997

Women

"I believe men and women are just genetically programmed to be incompatible"
Jim White, *Mojo*

The other piece of supreme irony is the inclusion on the defiant anti-love song *So Many Songs* of both of his ex-wives Kate McGarrigle and Suzzy Roche on backing vocals. Fiendish, some people would call it.
"Yeah, I thought that was pretty cute to have the Roches and the McGarrigles singing with me on the same track." he says, laughing. "It was funny in the studio—we took some snapshots and there's one of me laying on the ground and they're raising their feet as if they're about to stomp me to death. We still fight sometimes but we get along pretty well these days." So which one of them is *So Many Songs* about? "I'm not going to tell you that!...No it's about all the women I've ever loved..."
Colin Irwin, *Folk Roots* #19

You always go for very strong women, don't you?
"The weight-lifters in particular, yes"
Simon Bates, BBC Radio 2

Did you ever go in for counselling or any of that stuff at any stage of your life?
"Well I have seen a variety of shrinks. Shrinks and shamans, and fakirs, and, you know, massage artists. Yeah, I have a whole battery of people who've tried to take care of me. But it's those—I always wind up with those women instead!"
Simon Bates, BBC Radio 2

"My father gave me my first guitar. Actually there was a bit of a competition; he had a guitar and didn't take to it, or didn't learn how to play it or something. And between my brother and sister and me he said 'whoever learns to play this I'll give it to them'. He encouraged that kind of sibling rivalry and I jumped at the chance and I got the ax. I was 13 years old." K/BBC/89

Galway, September 1998

LWiii's wit is as dry as the Mojave and as sharp as the crease in a bond-trader's pants. His face is made of pure neoprene, and he's got the best comic timing in the singer-songwriter business

SG/S/07/96

About the Editors

Kevin Harrison and I met as students at Norwich School of Art in 1971. Although in different departments we had a shared affinity for the local greasy-spoon café where we met frequently over breakfast and discussed the meaning of life, and the relative merits of the mortise and tenon and the bridle joint.

Several years later entirely by coincidence we found ourselves living next door but one to one another in the east end of London. We became close friends, and have been ever since, collaborating from time to time in a variety of activities ranging from the creative to the mundane, and trying to amuse each other through the familiar traumas of contemporary life, including marriage, divorce and all the rest. I have an adult son and daughter, and Kevin three daughters.

Our shared interest in Loudon Wainwright began with another coincidence. Unknown to me, Kevin had been a Loudon fan for many years, and had every record he'd ever made. I chanced on an old tape of *T Shirt* one day while staying with some friends. I remembered Loudon Wainwright as a name that friends used to talk about in the early seventies, but hadn't thought about him since. For some reason I thought one or two tracks on the tape might appeal to Kevin and I sent him a copy, only then learning that Kevin had been an enthusiastic fan since Norwich Art School days. Kevin, in his turn, set about making up the deficit in my knowledge of Loudon's work, an eye-opener that converted me too into a serious enthusiast.

Kevin is a full-time sculptor and still lives in London. I now live in Dieppe, France where I publish *Breakfast All Day* , a little literary magazine.

PB

KH, LWiii and PB after one of Loudon's shows at the Hotel du Nord

Photo: Caesar Glebbeek ©

Loudon with Syd Shaw, Ronnie Scott's Club London, June 1999

Contacts and Websites

All enquiries about this book should be addressed to
SMMFS,
Studio 14,
64-68 Chisenhale Road,
London E3 5QZ
email: smmfs@badpress.com

Loudon Wainwright is represented by the
Rosebud Agency,
PO Box 170429, SF, CA 94117
Fax (415) 386 0599
Rosebudus@aol.com
http://www.rosebudus.com/wainwright/index.html

See also the following websites:

Ron Mura
http://www.wing.net/loudon/
email: rmura@world.std.com
Mailing list: majordomo@world.std.com

Martin Maguire's Belfast website
http://www.maguire22.freeserve.co.uk/loudon/
email:martin@maguire22.freeserve.co.uk

Kaare Myklebust
http://www.netpower.no/~kaarewm/LOUDONW3/
LOUDONW3.HTM
email:kaarewm@netpower.no

Sol Three
http://www.adios.demon.co.uk/lw3main.htm

Virgin
http://www.virginrecords.com/
artists/VR.cgi?ARTIST_NAME=Loudon_Wainwright

Notes

Quotations:
TJ/S   Ted Joseph, Sounds
BT/IOS   BenThompson, Independent on Sunday
DD/PL   Dan Deluca, Philadelphia Enquirer
NW/Times   Nigel Williamson, The Times
DH/Mojo   David Hepworth, Mojo
R O'D/MMM   Rob O'Dempsey, Musin' Music Mag
WR/Gold   William Ruhlman, Goldmine
BD/TO   Bruce Dessau, Time Out